A CRIME-SOLVING TOOLKIT

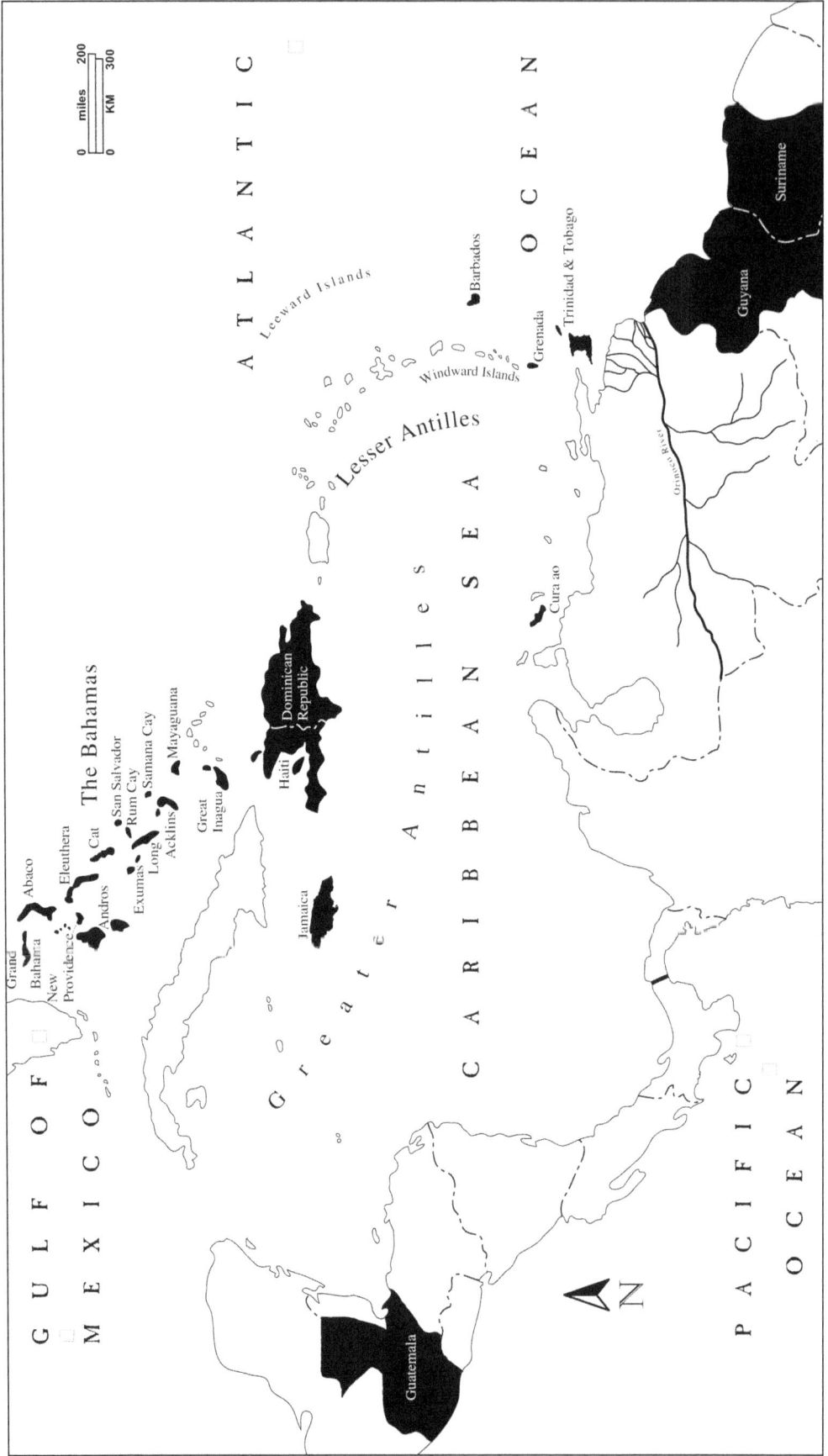

Caribbean and circum-Caribbean countries discussed in A Crime-Solving Toolkit: Forensics in the Caribbean

A CRIME-SOLVING TOOLKIT
Forensics in the Caribbean

Edited by

Basil A. Reid

University of the West Indies Press
Jamaica • Barbados • Trinidad and Tobago

University of the West Indies Press
7A Gibraltar Hall Road   Mona
Kingston 7   Jamaica
www.uwipress.com

13 12 11 10 09   5 4 3 2 1

A crime-solving toolkit : forensics in the Caribbean / edited by Basil A. Reid.

p. cm.

Includes bibliographical references.

ISBN: 978-976-640-220-4

1. Criminal investigation – Caribbean, English-speaking. 2. Forensic sciences –
Caribbean, English-speaking. 3. Crime scene – Caribbean, English-speaking.
4. Criminal investigation – Technological innovations. I. Reid, Basil A.

HV 8073.C84 2009   363.256

Book and cover design by Robert Harris.

Set in Sabon 10.5/15 x 27

Printed in the United States of America.

Contents

Foreword

JERRY **MELBYE**

WHEN MY GOOD FRIEND BASIL REID asked me to write a foreword for this book, I was not so sure I could do it. I knew enough about the geography and the political history of the Caribbean to appreciate that my knowledge was limited. However, I remembered a quote by Anton Chekhov: "There is no national science just as there is no national multiplication table; what is national is no longer science" (quoted in Kessler 2007).

In other words, there is no such thing as Caribbean forensic science. If you read the title of this book carefully, you will see that it is intended to be a compendium of the status of forensic science in the Caribbean, and that is exactly what it is.

As simply as I can put it, forensic science is the analysis of evidence for presentation in courts of law. It is the search for the true meaning of evidence without any prejudice, or presumption of guilt or innocence. This is the cornerstone of forensic science. Dr P.C.H. Brouardel, a French medico-legalist of the late nineteenth century expressed it eloquently: "If the law has made you a witness, remain a man of science – you have no victim to avenge, no guilty or innocent person to convict or save – you must bear testimony within the limits of science" (Hoyt 2006)

Forensic science also has many subdisciplines such as forensic entomology, forensic anthropology, forensic botany and so on. In the past, these specialists were called upon as simply scientists with an interest in bugs, bones, plants and so on. They had no idea of the depth, breadth, or protocols in the field of forensic science. We lived in "ivory towers" with little or no communication with each other. Today, it is quite different. We work together on cases and share information with each other to find the true meaning of evidence.

This book is a testimony to the modern approach of forensic scientists in the Caribbean. We begin with the newly developed plan for disaster management and protocols for mass fatalities. We also see that forensic anthropology can play an important role in the processing of suspicious deaths. Victim identification, time since death and perimortem trauma are some of the highlights.

Next we are treated to computer forensics: a rapidly expanding field. Increasingly, we are living in a digital world where enormous amounts of information are stored. Everything from child pornography to drug cartel records can be explored, retrieved and used in courts of law. The application of geospatial data in detecting "hot spots" in Jamaica is indeed an illuminating discourse on a very important issue. Shoe-print identification is an older, established method that is presented with the history of the field and its relationship to other subfields of forensic science. The next chapter focuses on to the use of forensic pathology in solving a suicide case in Sweden as well as its applicability to the Caribbean. The final chapter relates to the emerging field of forensic linguistics and this topic is explored in relation to witness testimony and language identification. This is a model article for any subfield of our science.

In summary, forensic science is alive and well in the Caribbean. There is ample evidence of cooperation, modern techniques, and dogged determination to find and present the truth in courts of law. The forensic scientist has an awesome responsibility as an expert witness. Regardless of who is paying us, our obligation is to the truth. We are not looking for evidence to support the prosecution or the defence; rather, we are on the side of the victim.

References

Hoyt, Constance A. 2006. Critical Care Preparatory Programs. *Critical Care Nursing Quarterly* 29 (3): 259–70. http://www.ccnq.com/pt/re/ccnq/abstract.00002727-200607000-0012.htm;jsessionid=Ly5DQLh209 Qshh8g9rTCBJdppVnymg41RKTmwxtPYqRJ gL16N3vF!542054210!181195628!8091!-1 (accessed October 5, 2008).

Kessler, Colleen. 2007. *Super Smart: Science*. Austin: Prufrock Press.

Acknowledgements

THIS VOLUME WOULD NOT HAVE BEEN possible without the sterling contributions of a number of individuals. First, I wish to thank the contributors for their chapters. I found them all to be both very interesting and highly informative. Not only do the chapters in this book reflect a wide breadth of knowledge, but they also provide useful insights into forensics within the context of the Caribbean. I am grateful to Jerry Melbye for writing the foreword and for providing constructive criticism during the project. Christopher A. Riley either scanned or drew images relating to chapter 2. He also converted a number of image files for other chapters. His contribution is gratefully acknowledged. I also wish to thank Naseema Hosein-Hoey, Alexandra Sajo, Maria Peter-Joseph and Shinelle Martin for providing general assistance, such as typing and collating some of the documents and contacting contributors. Linda Speth of the University of the West Indies Press deserves special commendation for her encouragement at every stage of this publication. Last but certainly not least, thanks to my lovely wife, Joan, and our son, Gavin, for their unflagging support, as I spent many hours editing and collating the seminal chapters of the book.

Forensics in the Caribbean

An Introduction

BASIL A. **REID**

EVEN THOUGH FORENSIC SCIENCES HAVE BEEN judiciously applied in the Caribbean for decades, the vast majority of forensics publications have tended to focus on North America and Europe with scant regard being paid to the Caribbean. This volume throws a wide perspective on forensics within the context of the Caribbean, as the topics stretch from mass fatality or disaster victim identification protocols, forensic anthropology, computer forensics and geospatial technologies, to shoe-print identification, suicide hangings and forensic linguistics. The topics also accurately reflect the rich diversity of the forensic sciences that can either be utilized or are currently being practised as an intrinsic part of the region's crime-solving toolkit.

Unacceptably high crime rates in the Caribbean continue to be a major preoccupation of policymakers, police departments, forensic science centres, tourism officials and ordinary Caribbean people, to the extent that Caribbean Community (CARICOM) governments, at the behest of their nationals, met in Port of Spain, Trinidad, in April 2008 to discuss issues of regional security. At the meeting, CARICOM agreed to take joint action against murders, kidnappings, drug trafficking and violent gangs in the region by upgrading and expanding the security arrangements that had been put in place during the 2007 Cricket World Cup. Among the measures were the Advanced Passenger Information System; the Regional Intelligence Fusion Centre in Port of Spain, which will coordinate the intelligence operations of all agencies throughout the region; and a Joint Regional Communications Centre. On the issue of murders, which have increased significantly in countries like Jamaica, Trinidad and Tobago, and Guyana, leaders agreed to develop specially trained, equipped and dedicated teams of homicide investigators; fully utilize forensics, including DNA; encourage comprehensive crime-scene management; and undertake the investigation and prosecution of accused persons in a timely manner. It is against this backdrop of mounting concerns about rising crime in the Caribbean, coupled with recent CARICOM proposals, that this book provides prescriptive formulas designed to mitigate the problem.

Chapter 1, by Cheryl Corbin, provides a useful discourse on mass fatality or disaster victim identification protocols for the Caribbean, predicated on a mock exercise at the Forensic Sciences Centre in Barbados. Corbin points out that one of the positive outcomes of the anglophone Caribbean hosting the International Cricket World Cup in 2007 was the greater emphasis placed on infrastructures relating to security, health and disaster management by venue countries. Based on a mock up exercise at the Forensic Sciences Centre in Barbados as well as real life situations, chapter 1 discusses the capabilities of the Forensic Sciences Centre of Barbados to meet mass fatality challenges wherever and whenever they occur. Mass fatality incidents can be natural (such as tsunamis, earthquakes and hurricanes), accidental (such as a building collapse or ship sinking) or can occur as a result of a terrorist attack. Terrorism alone has been responsible for thousands of deaths in recent years and can be encountered in many forms (such as suicide bombings and aeroplane hijackings). In mass fatality situations, the skills and expertise of many forensic specialists are required to assist in the identification efforts and to allow for the speedy return of recovered human remains to the relatives of the deceased (Graham 2006). While the Caribbean has never experienced natural disasters like the December 26, 2004, Indian Ocean tsunami or the September 11, 2001, terrorist attacks in New York, events in our past, such as the 1983 Maurice Bishop coup in Grenada, the 1990 Muslimeen insurrection in Trinidad and the 1978 murder-suicide of more than nine hundred people in Jonestown, Guyana, stand as poignant reminders of the need for forensic centres in the region to be fully capable of dealing with mass fatality incidents and disaster victim identification should the need arise. Corbin's exemplary case study from Barbados can therefore be a valuable frame of reference for other Caribbean territories.

Chapter 2 seeks to underscore the potential usefulness of forensic anthropology based on three cases of suspected suicide from Trinidad and Tobago, but it also places this discussion squarely within a Caribbean context by intermittently examining crime scenarios in Jamaica and Guyana – two countries other than Trinidad and Tobago that have been experiencing a growing number of homicides. I highlight the fact that although forensic anthropology has been standard practice in North America, Europe and some Latin American countries, this is hardly the case in the anglophone Caribbean. I therefore make a compelling case for it to be included in the crime-solving toolkit of the region, and the first step in this process would be to provide overseas training opportunities for interested individuals.

The three case studies from Trinidad and Tobago relate to skeletonized remains as described in popular media reports. Perhaps the forensic anthropologist's most valuable skill is familiarity with subtle variations in the human skeleton (Mann and Ubelaker 1990). Although most adult skeletons have the same number of bones (206), no two skeletons are identical. Therefore, observations of patterns or unique skeletal traits frequently lead to positive identifications. Skeletonized remains aside, an important point made in this chapter is that forensic anthropology can also be usefully applied in situations where bodies are decomposed, burned, mutilated or otherwise unrecognizable. A number of these cases have been reported in the local and regional media with alarming regularity (Charan 2008; *Newsday* 2006; Gayle and Sinclair 2007; Caleb-Browne 2008; "Guyana Under Siege" n.d.). Clearly, the skills and dexterity of forensic anthropologists can be effectively utilized in a variety of homicide contexts throughout the Caribbean. This further bolsters the argument that the region urgently needs its own cadre of forensic anthropologists to solve many of the heinous crimes that are being committed.

Chapter 3, by Sheau-Dong Lang and Nazir Alladin, and chapter 4, by Parris Lyew-Ayee, both showcase the use of computer technologies as important tools of forensic investigation. In Lang and Alladin's seminal chapter, which includes an interesting mix of Caribbean examples and a hypothetical case study, the spotlight is placed on sophisticated computer forensics tools with a graphical user interface. In their view, these tools more effectively handle larger amounts of disk storage and data. In addition, they have enabled forensic examiners to recover previously deleted files and folders, recognize disk partitions and common file systems (Windows FAT and NTFS, Linux ext2 and ext3, Unix UFS), carve graphics and other files of known signatures from unallocated disk clusters, search strings using regular expressions, review registry files (on Microsoft Windows systems), recover user passwords, recover e-mail and instant messages, provide timelines of file access activities based on date/time stamps, identify known files based on hash sets, and identify artefacts specific to the operating system on disk.

Lang and Alladin's chapter should resonate well with not only forensic specialists but also with popular audiences given that computers are now considered "run-of-the-mill" technology in many Caribbean countries. It is precisely because computers are so commonplace in the region that they are increasingly being used to perform criminal acts such as the production and distribution of child pornography, financial crimes, information and corporate espionage, exploitation, stalking, and identity theft (see Taylor et al. 2006). The opportunities to commit computer crime and the technical competence of the criminals have expanded faster than we can control them (ibid.). Caribbean countries, as Lang and Alladin correctly assert, are especially vulnerable to this level of transnational criminal intrusion because of their geography, small size, growing culture of corruption, general tardiness of response and lack of financial resources to keep pace with rapid technological advances.

One response to the increasing criminality in Jamaica is the growing use of geographic information systems (GIS) to map and identify areas in communities characterized by high crime rates, also known as "hotspots". Based on GIS applications, Parris Lyew-Ayee, in chapter 4, critically explores the spatial dimension of crime and the tools used to analyse crime patterns and trends. In this chapter, geospatial technologies are specifically used to map crime-ridden areas of Kingston, especially those "hot spots" south of Cross Roads. An important point made by Lyew-Ayee is that a purely technological solution, based on GIS technology, will not accomplish anything if it is not subject to careful analyses relating to the social, economic and political contexts of crime in Jamaica. Although the initial costs of GIS technology are usually quite high, once the data sets are generated they can become an important cost-saving tool in crime detection.

It is important to note that utilizing geospatial technologies is part and parcel of the rapidly emerging field of crime science that seeks to get upstream of crime and proactively prevent it, rather than merely respond to it. It is a radical departure from old ways of thinking about the problem of crime in society in which we respond after crimes are committed. The application of geospatial technologies in crime mapping and detection is well established in North America (Boba 2005; Rossmo 2000; Wang 2005) and Europe (*Directions Magazine* 2002; DGI Europe 2009). However, Lyew-Ayee's use of geospatial technologies in Jamaica is relatively new to the Caribbean. It therefore represents an important development in the region and can be used as a template by other Caribbean territories.

Although shoe-print identification is standard practice in North America and Europe, it is not as common in the Caribbean. In chapter 5, Trevor Modeste gives us rich insights into this technique, with much of the discussion coalescing around the crime scene of Beaureguard, Grenada, as well as the court case that followed. Modeste opens with a brief exposé on the application of footwear analysis in the United States and Europe. In this chapter, the author then recounts the incident at Beaureguard, his involvement in the case and its eventual outcome as adjudicated in a court of law. Modeste should be commended for recommending a slew of simple, very doable techniques in footwear identification that can be easily copied by police officers throughout the Caribbean. Prime examples of this are his detailed descriptions of how to process footwear and footprint impressions on hard, smooth and clean surfaces, polished wood, tiles, glass, and glazed floors. Overall, the procedures described in the chapter are meticulously presented and can act as a guide for future shoe identification cases in the Caribbean.

Chapter 6 is based on Carl Martin Winskog's article on an unusual suicide case from Sweden, the author's country of origin. This chapter, although premised on a case study from a European country far removed from the Caribbean, has important implications for the Caribbean because, like Sweden, suicides are fairly commonplace in particular Caribbean territories. With respect to Trinidad and Tobago, while most suicides are pesticide-induced, perpetrated by Indo-Trinidadians residing in south Trinidad, a significant number of suicides are the result of hanging. Over the years, there have also been hanging suicides reported in Jamaica and Barbados. Winskog's chapter offers an important cautionary tale about the dangers of misinterpreting critical forensic evidences when determining cause and manner of death.

Chapter 7, by Godfrey Steele, brings us to the issue of forensic linguistics. Forensic linguistics is the name given to a number of subdisciplines within applied linguistics that relate to the interface between language, the law and crime. Steele posits that although forensic linguistics is a well-established discipline in both the United Kingdom and the United States, where it has been frequently applied in myriad civil and criminal cases, it is relatively unknown in the Caribbean. This chapter explores, through a survey of cases reported in the Trinidad and Tobago media, the possibilities for engaging forensic linguists in the finding of facts in selected cases dealing with witness statements. It also furnishes concrete examples that can shed well-needed light on the nuanced interpretations of a language within a legal context in Trinidad and Tobago and the wider Caribbean.

Though scholarly books and journals are cited in references, due to the fledging nature of forensic research in the Caribbean, chapters 1, 2 and 7 have had to rely rather heavily on reports from popular media, especially newspaper articles, as sources of information. Citing popular media reports is not unusual in forensic studies for countries outside the Caribbean. For instance, in their study of the nature and incidence of homicide-suicide in the Netherlands from 1992 to 2005, Liem and Koenraadt (2007) used several cases reported in both national and regional newspapers. On the basis of newspaper accounts, Liem and Koenraadt revealed that (1) homicide-suicide in the Netherlands occurred on average seven times per year during this time period; (2) spousal/consortial homicide-suicide was predominant, followed by homicide-suicide involving the perpetrator's own children and familicide-suicide; (3) the perpetrators across all categories of homicide-suicide were predominantly male; (4) the victims were predominantly women and children; and (5) firearms were used in the majority of the homicides and subsequent suicides. Popular media reports can be utilized, provided that they contain reasonably accurate information. Further, *A Crime-Solving Toolkit: Forensics in the Caribbean* is a pioneering publication. As such, forensic books and articles specific to the Caribbean do not exist in great abundance.

This volume, probably the first of its kind in the Caribbean, represents an important milestone in scholarly research in the region. Its eclectic mix of essays, penned by authors of diverse academic or professional backgrounds, is reflective of a multiplicity of theoretical and methodological approaches, and will provide valuable nuggets of information for forensic specialists, lawyers, police officers, anthropologists, computer specialists, linguists and interested members of the public within and outside of the Caribbean.

References

Boba, Rachael L. 2005. *Crime Analysis and Crime Mapping.* London: Sage.

Caleb-Browne, A. Aisha. 2008. Suspicious Death: Man's Burnt Body Discovered in Jennings. *Antigua Sun.* February 20. http://www.antiguasun.com/paper/?as=view&sun=364521047102212008&an=293408087702202008&ac=Local (accessed October 4, 2008).

Charan, Richard. 2008. Body Snatchers. *Daily Express.* January 20. http://www.trinidadexpress.com/index.pl/article_news?id=161266726 (accessed May 9, 2008).

DGI Europe. 2009. The Fifth Annual European Geospatial Intelligence Conference (January 19–23, 2009). http://www.wbr.co.uk/dgieurope/ (accessed July 9, 2008).

Directions Magazine. 2002. InfoTech Europe Hits the Headlines. October 11. http://www.directionsmag.com/press.releases/index.php?duty=Show&id=5730&trv=1 (accessed July 9, 2008).

Gayle, Barbara, and Glenroy Sinclair. 2007. 2006 Year in Review: Police Gain Ground But Murders Still High. *Jamaica Gleaner*, January 15. http://www.jamaica-gleaner.com/gleaner/20070115/lead/lead9.html (accessed May 7, 2008).

Graham, E.A.M. 2006. DNA Reviews: Disaster Victim Identification. *Forensic Science Medicine and Pathology* 2 (3): 203–8.

"Guyana Under Siege". N.d. Brama and the Escapees. http://www.guyanaundersiege.com/Security/Deathsquad/Brama and the Escapees.htm (accessed May 7, 2008).

Liem, M.C.A., and F. Koenraadt. 2007. Homicide-suicide in the Netherlands: A study of Newspaper Reports, 1992–2005. *Journal of Forensic Psychiatry and Psychology* 19 (4): 482–93. http://www.informaworld.com/smpp/content~content=a782644487~db=al l~jumptype=rss (accessed July 9, 2008).

Mann, Robert W., and Douglas H. Ubelaker, 1990. The Forensic Anthropologist. *FBI Law Enforcement Bulletin* 59 (7): 20–23. Also available online at http://www.crimeandclues.com/forensicanthropologist.htm (accessed May 9, 2008).

Newsday. 2006. Bodies Found in Burnt Car. December 5, 4.

Rossmo, D. Kim. 2000. *Geographic Profiling.* Boca Raton: CRC Press.

Taylor, Robert W., Tory J. Caeti, D. Kall Loper, Eric J. Fritsch and John Liderbach. 2006. *Digital Crime and Digital Terrorism.* London: Pearson.

Wang, Fahui, ed. 2005. *Geographic Information Systems and Crime Analysis.* Hershey, PA: Idea Group Publishing.

Forensic Protocols in Disaster Victim Identification

A Caribbean Perspective

CHERYL A. **CORBIN**

Abstract

Every year the Caribbean region prepares for the hurricane season. The regional governments are responsible for the design of disaster management and mass casualty plans, but most islands do not possess mass fatality or disaster victim identification protocols. In 2007, for the first time ever, the International Cricket World Cup was hosted by the English-speaking Caribbean. This event encouraged the venue countries to upgrade their infrastructure, and emphasis was placed on security, health and disaster management. The Forensic Sciences Centre bore the responsibility for the design of the mass fatality and disaster victim identification protocols in Barbados. Highlighted in this chapter are the major protocol elements that accentuate pre-planning, simulations, quality control and information communication technology systems. The chapter also discusses the critical forensic services that must be deployed efficiently after activation. This information should assist the reader in better understanding the essential operations of forensic protocols in disaster victim identification and the pitfalls to be avoided in the future.

Introduction

The Caribbean region prepares for the hurricane season every year and therefore regional governments are responsible for the design and implementation of disaster management and mass casualty plans. In

2007, for the first time, the Caribbean hosted the International Cricket Council Cricket World Cup. This major event prompted the national planners to upgrade their infrastructure and emphasis was placed on security, health and disaster management. It became evident that most Caribbean territories did not possess mass fatality plans, but and there were few written standard operating procedures specifically targeting mass fatality or disaster victim identification. There are a variety of disaster management and mass fatality plans available worldwide, from the US Disaster Mortuary Operational Response Team procedures to the Interpol disaster victim identification guide. These can provide a useful frame of reference for the Caribbean. It would be wise to utilize this existing body of information as a benchmark for developing specific plans for the region. This chapter provides some basic information and guidelines on the preparation of an effective plan suited to the uniqueness of the Caribbean.

The Forensic Sciences Centre, Office of the Attorney General, is responsible for the design of the mass fatality and disaster victim identification protocols in Barbados. To achieve an appropriate working model there are many factors to consider, and some of these will be presented step-wise with examples from the operational experiences and documents formulated by the centre. The reader should therefore appreciate that the material contained herein demonstrates the unique profile of the disaster victim identification and mass casualty capacity of the Caribbean region.

Disaster Management and Mass Casualty Plans

In some circles, elements of the mass fatality plan are incorporated near the end of the mass casualty plan. The Forensic Sciences Centre took the position that two separate documents would be prepared where the mass fatality plan speaks to the mass casualty plan but either protocol could be activated in its own right. A mass casualty incident is defined as an event, which generates, or has the potential to generate, sufficient victims to overwhelm the existing emergency services' ability to adequately manage patients. In Barbados this threshold has been set at twelve victims. Historically, in Barbados the management of fatalities arising out of a mass casualty incident has had limited forensic analytical input largely due to the lack of forensic capacity on the island. With the establishment of the Forensic Sciences Centre and the expansion of its range of services, the national competence in forensic investigations has significantly improved. The centre also offers assistance in this regard to any of the neighbouring islands that require it. Furthermore, the urgent need for any national strategy in the Caribbean should be viewed within the wider context of the international community moving towards a more structured approach in which there is better management of large-scale disasters, including the capacity to utilize foreign resources in such eventualities.

In developing a mass casualty plan, the principles of victim identification, as acknowledged in the Interpol-published document *Disaster Victim Identification Guide 1997*, can form the basis of the strategy and can serve to inform future modifications to both victim identification and the national strategy on disasters. The Interpol document is based on practical experiences gained from actual incidents and the guidelines presented can be modified by countries to conform to national or regional laws and regulations, or to religious or organizational practices. The document describes general aspects of disaster handling, integrated operation by several experts and the three major stages of victim identification, namely procurement of ante-mortem data, recovery and examination of the bodies, and the comparison of information taken prior to death and that taken after death, as it relates to each victim.

Disasters, whether natural, technological or man-made, are unfortunately a fact of life, and they precipitate investigations that involve police, forensic, medical and technical personnel.

A mass fatality plan, based on the following structure, is therefore required:

1. Introduction
2. Purpose or scope
3. Memoranda of understanding
4. Welfare, activation and related mechanisms
5. Recovery and collection
6. Identification and notification
7. Debriefing
8. Final report

The introduction should speak to the country's demographics and background as well as to any vulnerability, whether internal or external, that exists or is highly probable. Certain major assumptions also have to be identified; for example, does the country have an existing disaster management agency, and does a plan exist? It is critical to keep in mind that the islands of the Caribbean have limited physical, human and financial resources, and it would not be realistic to expect our operations to be on the same scale as those of larger, developed nations.

The purpose or scope identifies the objective of the plan which should be specific to the country of focus. This is fundamental to our success in preparing documents that define parameters relating to the mass casualty plan such as administrative, security, rescue, legal factors and methods of notification.

In recent years, the Caribbean islands have experienced relatively few mass fatalities compared to other developed or larger countries in the world. The intention is not to diminish the severity and emotional impact of other nations' misfortunes, but it is important that we learn from them. One of the first lessons is the necessity of rapid response from and cooperation between both local governmental and non-governmental agencies. The nature of the disaster dictates the operational activities required. For example, if a country experiences an earthquake that results in a landslide engulfing a number of homes, the initial actions taken by the disaster management team will be dictated by the assessment, and the resulting response will be specific to this category of disaster. It therefore becomes critical for the authority developing the plan to be cognizant of the variations in design that need to be made to support different types of incidences. For example, in Barbados on August 27, 2008, an apartment block collapsed into an underground cave, resulting in the land in the immediate vicinity of the impact becoming unstable. As a result, the responders could not venture to the edge of the cliff and had to utilize a crane with a very long boom arm to hoist personnel up and over the edge to assess the damages.

The geographical isolation of an area determines the speed with which the responders can get into the area in order to provide emergency assistance while simultaneously doing an assessment of needs. This was very evident in May 2004, when a remote village named Mapou, Haiti, and the neighbouring town of Jimani in the Dominican Republic, were flooded. Over nine hundred people died and the flood waters not only stalled rescuers from getting into the area, but also aid workers who wished to provide assistance to the survivors. The potential of the spread of malaria and dengue was of paramount concern along with the recovery and disposal of bodies since rivers of mud were hindering the operations.

In times of national crises, precipitated by disasters, it is customary for all available persons to come to the aid of the victims and to lend assistance wherever possible. It is prudent therefore for the national authority to secure appropriate arrangements with both governmental and non-governmental agencies to ensure an implementation strategy that is effective and efficient. A memoranda of understanding between the national authority and any other assisting body is critical to the process and should therefore ensure that

- the mechanism of cooperation between the national disaster management authority and all other agencies is properly devised;
- there are mandatory requirements to allow the smooth implementation of the plan, namely, training and financial resources and so on;
- there is adequate legal infrastructure within which governmental and non-governmental agencies can operate; and
- there is application of costing systems, reimbursement procedures as well as the injection of sufficient financial resources.

Prior to activation, the overall strategy of the plan must be fully understood by all involved. The welfare of personnel must be considered at the earliest. The health and safety of the first responders, the family of the deceased and the support staff are of paramount importance. Both a responsible authority and liaison should be identified. The mechanism for their operation as well as a location from which the dissemination of the information will be facilitated must be provided.

In the majority of the Caribbean islands, the incident command is managed by the police force, in collaboration with other pertinent agencies like the offices for disaster management, the fire service, defence forces and other members of the government's executive. Each agency usually possesses a set of rules for activation when operating independently, but it is essential that all of these mechanisms be well integrated into the respective country's national disaster management plan.

There are vital requisites for the efficient and effective coordination of the national plan.

Leadership: Definitive legislation and policy decisions on the appropriate role of the coordinating institution or institutions.

Oversight committee: Active representation of directors of each lead agency.

Determination of intervention priorities: Activation of certain elements of the plan dependent on the types of incident.

Prevention of duplicate effort: Identification of roles and responsibilities of players to ensure all needs are met and that each player is given specific tasks.

Communication: Utilization of technology for effective communication.

Development of uniform policies: Common standards and guidelines should apply to the entire process.

The Interpol Disaster Victim Identification Guide delivers a strategy matrix that can be modified for use to meet national requirements.

The organizational planning can be divided into three main categories: communications, rescue/recovery and disaster victim identification. There should be an investigator in charge of all three categories, and he or she is expected to collate the status reports as well as communicate with public relations and the executive operating centre where the policymakers and ministerial officials reside. The communications coordinator ensures that all transmissions between the primary responders as well as to the external agencies are dealt with evenly, securely and efficiently. The network for transmissions would include VHF, UHF, cellular and landline phones, facsimile, Internet, e-mail, telex, and dispatch.

The director of rescue/recovery operations liaises with the onsite manager who is resident at a command centre and manages the team leaders working in the areas of security, rescue, medical assistance, crime-scene management, search, recovery and transportation as well as victim identification.

The Disaster Victim Identification Process (General Principles)

There are three primary stages of operation within the disaster victim identification process:

1. **Collection of ante-mortem information:** This biological database of the victim, prior to death, includes physical characteristics, biological or medical conditions, and items from their personal effects

from which a DNA profile can be obtained. Related information from maternal or paternal family members is also very useful. Ante-mortem data sources also include existing medical and dental records which may be found in databases of a military, volunteer, identity, criminal and DNA nature and also historic photographs, current media and other visual aids. The police handle the collection and coordination of the information, and a liaison desk and officer are usually established to facilitate this exercise. Families and friends are encouraged to produce photos for visual identification; toothbrushes, combs and brushes for gathering of DNA; and any other information that may be of assistance to the investigation.

2. **Recovery and examination of bodies for reliable post-mortem evidence:** The victims are delivered to the mortuary, or, in the Barbados situation, the Forensic Sciences Centre and the forensic pathologist and his team perform an autopsy and complete forensic investigations on the body. In Barbados and most Commonwealth territories, the primary responsibility of the pathologist, based on the Coroner's Act, is to determine the cause of death. The pathologist also assists the law enforcement agency in the identification of the victim by removing tissue samples for DNA analysis, facilitating the taking of fingerprints and the cataloguing of any physical characteristics that may contribute to the subject's uniqueness.

3. **Comparison of ante-mortem to post-mortem data towards the final identification of the victim:** The information gathered is collated in the ante-mortem/post-mortem database, PLASSDATA which was designed by Interpol. Accuracy in identification is achieved by matching ante-mortem to post-mortem data from the following:

   - Dental records
   - Fingerprints
   - DNA profiles
   - Medical conditions
   - Circumstantial evidence (personal effects)
   - Visual identification

The Interpol disaster victim identification guide stipulates that visual identification is not a primary standard, as it lends itself to gross inaccuracy, especially where disfigurement is a factor. It may also lead to serious embarrassment, distress for families and cause legal difficulties. It is vital that accurate identification is achieved by evaluating a combination of objective scientific criteria that can be gleaned from the examination of dental records, fingerprints and DNA profiles. Physical evidence is extremely useful in the identification process. This includes general features such as gender, age, height and size and also unique features such as fingerprints, dental and lost limbs. These features can be combined with extraordinary features like scars, moles, tattoos and piercing, thereby contributing to a positive identification of the deceased.

Internal physical evidence retrieved as a result of post-mortem observations – lack of internal organs, evidence of previous surgeries, medical conditions – can be matched with the medical records provided as part of the ante-mortem data. Toxicological or clinical findings, revealing evidence of drugs (prescription/ abuse), poisons, carbon monoxide, and possible HIV status, can also contribute valuable information. Histological findings of tissue (necrosis, cancer), dental findings – teeth, jaw bone characteristics, dentures and implants – and, of course, genetic matching in the form of DNA profiling, are all invaluable to the process. It should be noted that DNA can be used effectively to match limbs or body parts to persons, but attempts to link victims to parents may involve the risk of proving non-paternity.

Disaster victim identification comprises two main lines of investigation – police and scientific. Many countries undertake forensics under the umbrella of local police departments. In Barbados, the lead scientific agency, which is not under the administration of the police, is the Forensic Sciences Centre, and it is under the aegis of the Office of the Attorney General. The chief executive officer of the centre is the director, and she leads a cadre of scientists, information specialists, quality personnel and administrative support staff in the daily operations of the department. The remainder of this chapter will focus on the work done at the Forensic Sciences Centre in Barbados in relation to the various steps involved in disaster victim identification.

The Forensic Sciences Centre in Barbados and Disaster Victim Identification

The centre has authored a mass casualty response plan, and key components of this plan will be highlighted here. The plan is executed in two phases, namely phase 1 and phase 2. During phase 2, all of the officers in the various departments of the centre may be required to lend support. However, during phase 1 the personnel from those sections cited below are usually the first key responders.

Security: Security personnel have the responsibility of protecting both the perimeter of the centre's compound as well as the building. It is also their responsibility to manage and coordinate communication within the Forensic Sciences Centre during a mass casualty incident.

Administration: The functions of the administrative staff, including the director and the deputy director, range from the overall management of the resources of the centre by senior management to issuing directives to more junior staff.

Evidence: Evidence officers are responsible for the entering of all data collected after receiving bodies.

Information systems: Information systems personnel lend technical support, as needed, to ensure that there is the uninterrupted flow of information via the information communication technology systems, network and telephones.

Maintenance: The maintenance coordinator, along with the sectional team, will provide janitorial support and minor maintenance of general equipment. The coordinator is also responsible for coordinating the involvement of external service providers.

Pathology: This is perhaps the most critical of all sections within the centre during the management of an incident, as it is responsible for coordinating the required forensic services. The pathologist is responsible for coordinating the examination of all bodies received, including performing autopsies.

Quality and chemical control: The quality section provides logistical support throughout the execution of this mass casualty response plan and is responsible for sourcing the requisite equipment and supplies for effective and efficient conduct of this exercise.

In accordance with the Government of Barbados's National Mass Casualty Management Plan 2006, the centre's response is managed under the incident command system and is activated whenever the Forensic Sciences Centre is alerted of a mass casualty incident. The plan is divided in two phases.

Phase 1: Phase 1 is the first segment of the plan concerned with the activation of the centre, the subsequent activities and the receipt of bodies. This phase is subdivided into alerting, mobilization, victim receipt, stand-down and debriefing. The alert is initiated by the Department of Emergency Management, and the centre must be given information on the requested alert status, that is, standby or activation, the location and scale of the incident, the anticipated number of bodies and their condition, approximate time of arrival, and method of transport (for example, civilian vehicle under police escort).

The mobilization of resources of the Forensic Sciences Centre pertain to resources such as personnel, equipment and supplies needed for the exercise. Once staff have been mobilized, they are briefed, and it is at this time that the sourcing and allocation of equipment and supplies are undertaken. Upon being notified of an incident, the director (incident commander of centre) must review the information and determine the level of alert status; which may either be standby awaiting further information or full activation. The director must also make a decision as to the level of response necessary within the organization itself.

The director then briefs the staff, and if the notification occurs during normal working hours, all routine work must be suspended in the shortest time possible. Victim receipt is the primary objective of phase 1 and can only be initiated if the alert status communicated is activation. Prior to this, all other activities may occur in either a stand-by or activation status. It is during this phase that bodies are transported to the centre, recorded, tagged with a unique identifier and stored.

During a mass casualty incident, it is anticipated that bodies may be transported to the Forensic Sciences Centre, directly from the scene of the incident under the escort of uniformed members of either the national police or defence force. In accordance with the Coroner's Act, the agency delivering the victims must be in possession of documentation that clearly states their authorization to transport these bodies to the centre.

Upon arriving at the centre's compound, the names and identification of the driver and passenger(s) of the vehicle are provided to the security personnel. The driver provides a count of the number of bodies being transported. The security guard completes the relevant entry/visitor reports and directs the driver to the delivery point where the bodies will be offloaded and tagged. The receiver must tally the total number of bodies from each vehicle and record it on the relevant portion of the form which must be returned to the driver with instructions to hand the slip to the security personnel at the exit point. From this point, bodies may be directed either immediately into storage or to the examination area in order to facilitate the victim identification process.

The decision to place bodies in storage before they are examined should be made by the designated leader of the pathology team in discussions with the director. This decision will be based on the condition of the bodies, the available personnel resources, the number of bodies being received and the national situation. In all instances, the decision must weigh in favour of preserving the body in the best condition possible with the minimum deterioration. Therefore the "default" position will be that bodies are tagged and directed to storage pending updates on the circumstances that precipitated the mass casualty incident. On receipt of the stand-down notification (that is, instructions to return to normal operations when the mass casualty incident is over), the director will as soon as possible request a report on the status of the operation from the leader of the pathology team. The stand-down notification for the centre will be communicated once all bodies have been properly stored, even if examination activities continue. Once this announcement is given, the director shall indicate the time and location of the debriefing. The debriefing of all persons involved must occur prior to the initiation of phase 2. It is an important compulsory component of this plan. A report must be presented by all section leaders who participated in the exercise and must encompass all aspects of the activity, from the alerting to the stand-down. The report should highlight any challenges encountered, measures taken to overcome those challenges and suggestions for improvement going forward. The debriefing will also provide a useful frame of reference for phase 2 activities.

Phase 2: In addition to the debriefing that occurs at the end of phase 1, there must be constant updates during the implementation of phase 2. Phase 2 signals the examination of bodies, both to identify the victim and to determine cause of death, and may immediately follow the conclusion of phase 1 or be initiated at a later date, dependant on individual circumstances or on instructions received from the coroner. The mode of operation will be decided on by the director with input from the pathologist and other key technical staff.

An important component of victim identification is the viewing of bodies by family members. It must be noted that this phase of the process will not begin until the initial emergency status has been suspended and all bodies have been processed at least as far as storage. Counselling support is provided for families and friends of the deceased as required. The Forensic Sciences Centre already provides this type of support, but the overall welfare coordinator, who may be in the employ of the Department of Emergency Management, should be responsible for the programme.

The Forensic Sciences Centre continues to develop the existing plans as dictated by current trends in Barbados as well as the prevailing standards of the Interpol Disaster Victim Identification Standing Committee. The management of the centre recognizes that the only way to sustain this level of preparedness is to undertake departmental and national table-top or field-based simulations at least twice a year.

Disaster Victim Identification Simulation

In January 2006, the centre embarked on its first simulation exercise in the preparations for Cricket World Cup 2007. The exercise surrounded a staging of a collapsed spectator stand resulting in a mass casualty (figures 1.1, 1.2 and 1.3).

The incident command system was used and the figures below present the sequence of activities that were undertaken by the personnel of the centre and the Barbados Defence Force.

Figure 1.1
Casualties arrive with a Barbados Defence Force escort

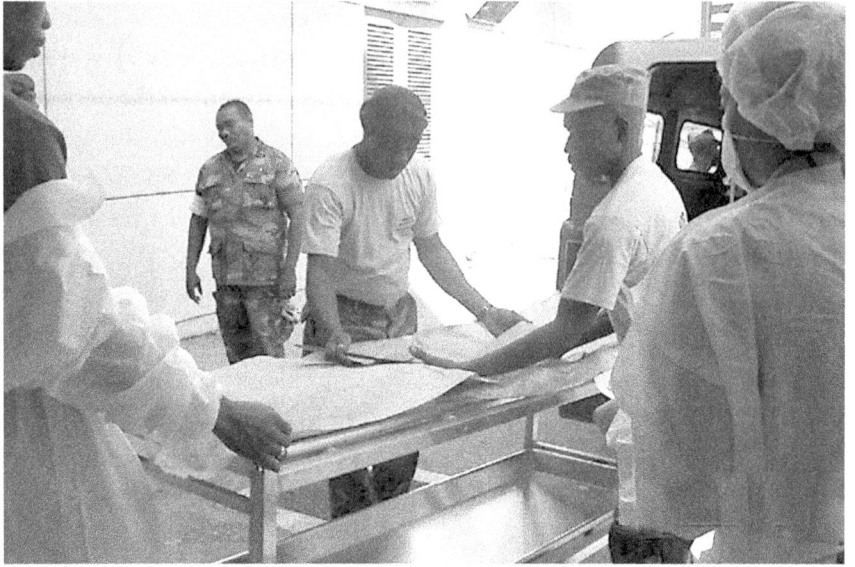

In accordance with the national disaster management protocol and the centre's mass casualty plan, the activation notification was received, and personnel assembled at the centre's command point for the initial briefing. The circumstances surrounding the incident were relayed, with all officers in charge being required to move in their respective sections to complete the final checks, thereby ensuring absolute readiness to receive the first bodies.

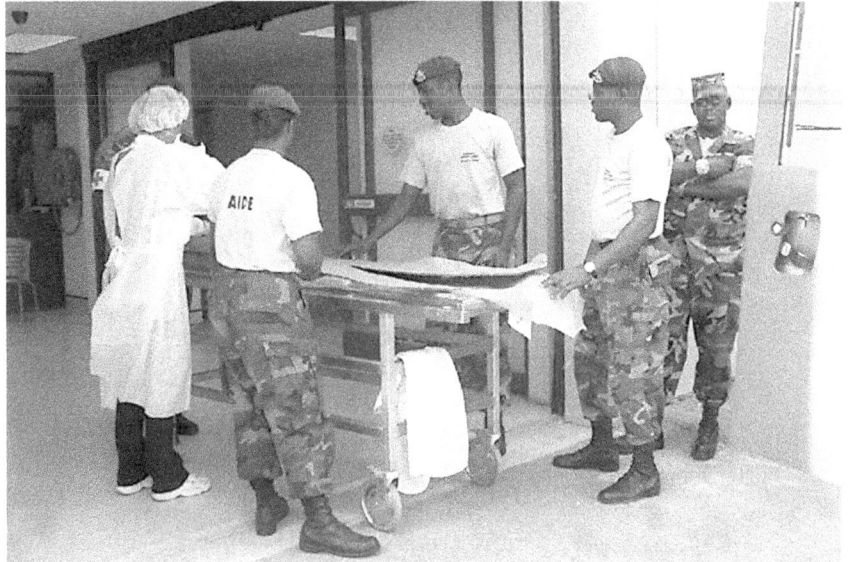

For the purpose of the simulation, the casualties included cardboard cut-outs and "walking dead" (persons pretending to be fatalities). The vehicles that delivered the deceased were recorded by security and ushered to the delivery point. Here the offloading and initial cataloguing by the centre's body receivers was conducted. The Barbados Defence Force delivered the victims, and even though many of them were not "human", they were dealt with professionally and with sensitivity.

At the time of the simulation, the decision was taken to process the bodies immediately after they were received. However, upon reviewing the exercise, it was determined that there were certain elements that were performed too hastily. It became evident that once the receipt and cataloguing of bodies had been completed, it was more important to secure the bodies, await the stand-down notification, and gather all relevant information from the police and associated agencies that directly impacted on the disaster victim identification process. The centre therefore amended the protocols to create a matrix that supported a phase 1 and phase 2, as described earlier. One major lesson learned from the simulation was that we should not be overly anxious to perform procedures that ought to be done in a timely manner (figures 1.4, 1.5 and 1.6). The separation into the two phases allowed for a more focused operation, hence a greater chance at success in the investigation.

At the outset, it was stated that the formulation of the mass casualty plan was driven by Barbados's preparations for the Cricket World Cup

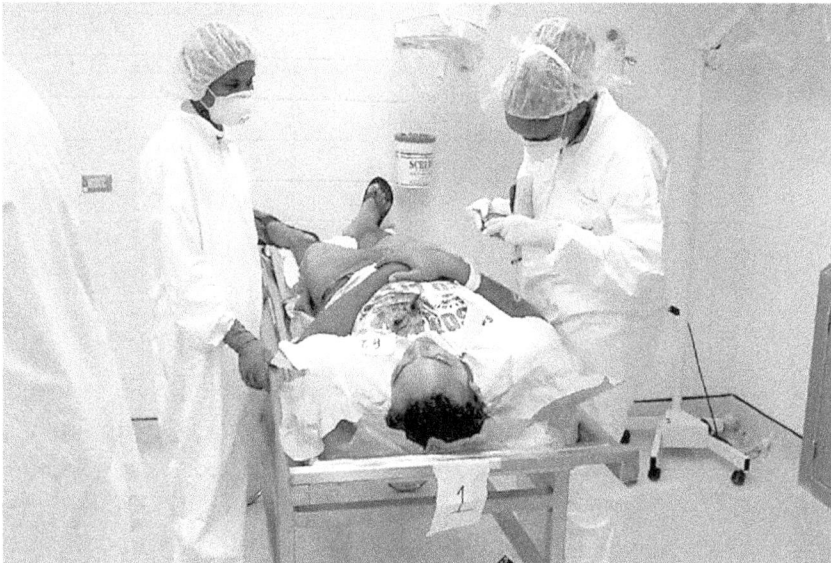

Figure 1.4
Initial cataloguing of victims (including their external injuries)

Figure 1.5
Cataloguing continues

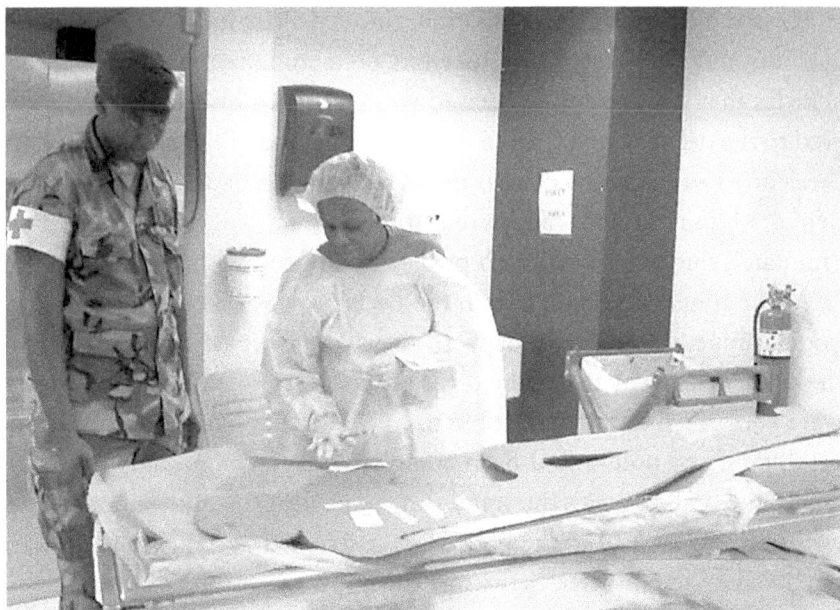

Figure 1.6
Preparing to secure body in freezer bay

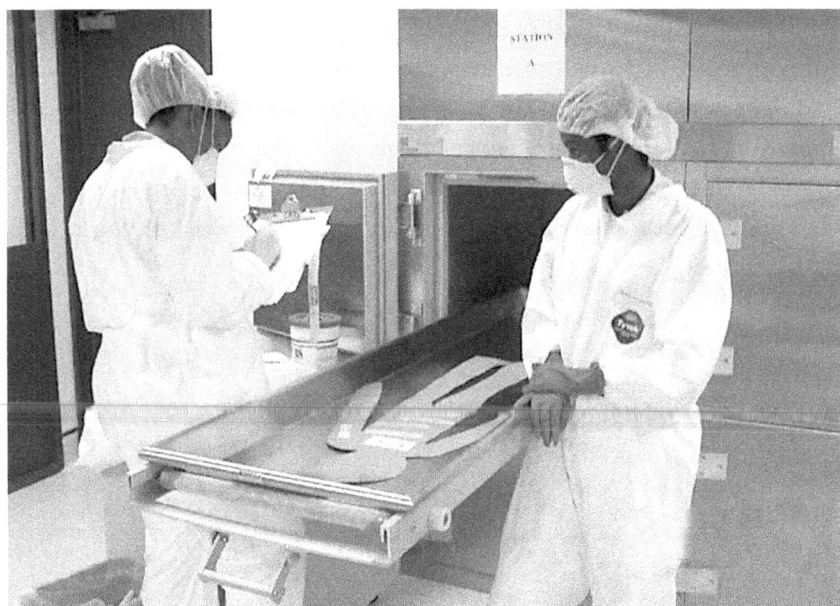

in 2007. Arguably, therefore, one of the legacies of this international sporting event is the implementation of national mass casualty systems for the Caribbean region. Given the many specific accidents and natural disasters affecting the Caribbean over the years, this is indeed relevant and timely. A few examples are discussed below.

1. Post–West Indies World Cup

The objective of the mass casualty management system is to maximize existing resources as well as to facilitate effective multi-agency preparation and responses with strong pre-planning and coordination. In Barbados, the response plan was successfully implemented on four separate occasions within six months of the final Cricket World Cup games. The first incident took place in May 2007 when thirteen people were injured in Coach Hill, St John, as two public transport buses collided. There were no fatalities, and persons with minor injuries were treated on the spot.

2. Tour Bus Crash at Joes River, St Joseph

Just after 11 o'clock on the morning of July 29, 2007, the lives of three men and three women were cut short when a forty-seater vehicle carrying patrons, who had purchased an all-inclusive package from Mount Gay Distilleries (for the much-anticipated and high-paced Crop Over Party Monarch Finals), was involved in an accident. The accident caused an additional thirty-seven persons to seek medical attention at the Accident and Emergency Department of the Queen Elizabeth Hospital. The six bodies were delivered to the centre directly from the scene of the accident, and the autopsies and victim identifications were performed in accordance with the centre's protocols. The exercise was completed within three days; this was four days short of the customary one-week turnaround for this number of examinations.

3. Accident in Mullins Road, St Peter

On August 1, 2007, a small van carrying five persons collided with a much larger public service vehicle on a main road in the northern parish of Barbados. Four persons died, including one female adult and three children. The driver of the van escaped without major injuries. The bodies were delivered to the centre and the victim identification process was conducted with all ante-mortem data being reconciled with the positive identifications and post-mortem data.

4. Apartment Block Caves in at Arch Cot Terrace, Britton's Hill, St Michael

In the early hours of the morning of August 26, 2007, an apartment block collapsed in an underground cave and a family of five was feared

Figure 1.7
*The magnitude of
the cave-in*

Figure 1.8
*Impact of the cave-
in on the apartment*

to be dead. The national emergency response teams arrived quickly to the site, including the director and the pathologist of the centre. The area of the cave-in was quite vast (as can be seen in figures 1.7 and 1.8), and there was a major concern about the instability of the surrounding zone.

After the first few hours on site, an airborne assessment was conducted by hoisting rescuers on the boom arm of a large crane over the rubble. The information received from the aerial visual inspection was

factored into the rescuers' decision to go into the impact site (figure 1.9). The bodies were recovered within five days of the collapse and were all positively identified by the Forensic Sciences Centre's team, utilizing the foregoing disaster victim identification protocols.

Conclusion

Due to its level of preparedness, the Government of Barbados was able to manage these incidents with a great level of efficiency. Prior to 2007, the multi-agency approach and the cooperation between authorities were not as evident as after the World Cup event. Each agency did have their in-house protocols, but bringing this to a national stage where they all worked together as a team represented a new chapter in the development of the national mass casualty system. There were many lessons that were learned by all parties, such as the need to identify the roles and responsibilities of their individual agency personnel within the national matrix. There was a realization of a vital need to communicate with the victims' families as events unfolded. The medical officials and security and safety personnel, through their respective spokespersons, provided frequent updates to keep all apprised of developments.

Security personnel deftly instituted proper crowd control in the aftermath of the incident and received few complaints from the onlookers, many of whom were appreciative and supportive of the challenging tasks being undertaken by the forensic recovery teams. The discussion of the disaster management and mass casualty plans and disaster victim identification in this chapter has not been exhaustive. The capacity of various anglophone Caribbean states to adopt these proposals is contingent on how many trained people we have at our disposal, as well the level of funding available for sustaining such plans. This chapter suggests that some of these problems could be effectively tackled by the willingness of some countries to share information, skills and expertise with their Caribbean neighbours.

It is hoped that, from the foregoing discussion, the reader would have acquired a better understanding of the advantages and potential pitfalls to be avoided in the creation of a strategy for processing mass casualties. Participation in simulation exercises is invaluable and should always be incorporated into the planning framework. The case studies are useful demonstrations of these techniques' applicability within the Caribbean context. There is an old adage: "To be forewarned is to be forearmed." It is hoped that this information will be used to assist in designing similar programmes throughout the region.

References

Government of Barbados. 2006. *National Mass Casualty Management Plan 2006*. Bridgetown: Government of Barbados.

International Police Criminal Organization. 1997. *Interpol: Disaster Victim Identification Guide, 1997*. http://www.interpol.int/Public/DisasterVictim (accessed January 24, 2008).

Pan American Health Organization (PAHO). N.d. *Management of Dead Bodies after Disasters: A Field Manual for First Responders*. http://publications.paho.org (accessed January 24, 2008).

2

Forensic Anthropology
Applications in Trinidad and Tobago

BASIL A. **REID**

Forensic anthropology is the application of both the sciences of physical anthropology and human in a legal setting, most often in criminal cases where the victim's remains are more or less skeletonized. Although well established in both North America and Europe, the discipline of forensic anthropology is not yet widely practised in the anglophone Caribbean. However, with the rising criminal activity in the region, especially in larger territories like Jamaica, Guyana, and Trinidad and Tobago, there is a pressing need to add forensic anthropology to the arsenal of forensic techniques already at our disposal. By focusing on three cases of suspected homicides as reported in the local media of Trinidad and Tobago, this chapter explores how forensic anthropology can be usefully applied as an intrinsic part of the Caribbean's crime-solving toolkit. In order to underscore the potential usefulness of forensic anthropology for Trinidad and Tobago and the wider anglophone Caribbean, this chapter will be interspersed with illuminating case studies from both the United States and Canada.

Forensic Anthropology as Practised Outside the Caribbean

Although well established in both North America (Fairgrieve 1999a; Steadman 2003a) and Europe (Brickely and Ferlini 2007), forensic anthropology is not yet widely practised in the anglophone Caribbean, despite the fact that countries like Jamaica, the Bahamas, Trinidad and

Tobago, and Barbados possess government-funded forensic science centres. This has also been the case despite the relatively long practice of forensic anthropology in both the circum-Caribbean and South America. In 1984, investigations by Eric Stover and a team of forensic scientists from the American Association for the Advancement of Science led the exhumation of mass graves in a search for the disappeared in Argentina. This heralded the beginning of forensic anthropology in that country (Stover and Ryan 2001). In Guatemala, the use of forensic anthropology was established in 1991 and has continued to the present, where only relatively recently (since 1998) have individuals been brought to trial and the anthropological evidence heard in court. Both Argentina and Guatemala have established permanent national forensic teams as a result of the early training they received during these investigations (Simmons and Haglund 2005).

The rising number of homicides in the anglophone Caribbean, particularly in Jamaica, Guyana, and Trinidad and Tobago, dictate that forensic anthropology be seriously considered as a viable crime-solving technique. In January 2008, gunmen shot and killed eleven people, including women and children still in bed, in the small village of Lusignan in Guyana, eleven miles east of Georgetown. The massacre came hours after gunmen attacked police headquarters in the capital, Georgetown. The television described the attackers as fugitive criminals (Khan 2008). In Jamaica, five bodies and two human skulls were discovered by the police in 1996 near the train line at Industrial Terrace in West Kingston (*Jamaica Newsweekly* 2007). In January 2006, skeletonized human remains, comprised of three skulls and several bones, were also found in the same area, leading the Jamaican police to speculate that criminals may have used this area as an "execution chamber" (ibid.). Also in Jamaica, on February 6, 2008, two skeletal remains, believed to be those of two children who went missing seven months before, were found in bushes off the Flint River main road in Hanover by a farmer, who was walking through the area (Frater 2008). The remains, which consisted of two skulls, leg and arm bones, and rib bones, were found alongside two half-buried pairs of shoes, a handbag, a silver chain, a hairpiece, a shirt, jeans shorts and a CD. They were found in an area covered with dried leaves and shrubs (ibid.). In December 2006, the Trinidad and Tobago police found the bodies of two men who were burned to death in a car in Guapo. A trail of blood led investigators to the burned-out car. Detectives believed that the men were kidnapped, killed and then burned (*Trinidad Guardian* 2006). In June 2007, the Trinidad and Tobago police found the bones of a woman who vanished in April of the same year while walking to Bible classes at her church (*Trinidad Daily Express* 2007). These are just a few examples that underscore the growing rate of criminality in the region as well as the concomitant need for additional forensic expertise.

This chapter will explore specific ways in which forensic anthropology can be usefully applied. Three homicide cases in Trinidad and Tobago, as described in media reports, will be central to the discussion. Police reports were unavailable to the author during the writing of this chapter and therefore could not be utilized as a primary database. It is important to note that there is already precedence for incorporating media reports into scholarly forensic publications (Liem and Koenraadt 2007). The argument for forensic anthropology in the Caribbean will also be supported by case studies drawn intermittently from both the United States and Canada. First, however, given its centrality to the chapter, a definition of forensic anthropology is required.

Forensic Anthropology Defined

Referred to as forensic archaeology in the United Kingdom (Hunter and Cox 2005), forensic anthropology is the branch of applied physical anthropology concerned with the identification of human remains and associated skeletal trauma related to the cause and manner of death in a legal context (Reichs 1998). It can also be defined as the application of anthropological and skeletal biological principles to medicolegal issues (Steadman 2003a, 2). The term "medicolegal" refers to the capability of medical science to shed light on legal matters, such as the identity of the deceased and circumstances of death (ibid.; Fisher 1993). Therefore, the forensic anthropologist is expected to be knowledgeable about osteology (skeletal anatomy and biology) as well as archaeological techniques invariably used in the recovery of human remains. While most forensic pathologists are accustomed to examining corpses with the flesh and tissues relatively intact, forensic anthropologists are specially trained to extract information by analysing human skeletons.

Although skeletonized remains are the primary focus of forensic anthropology, the forensic anthropologist is also trained to identify deceased individuals whose remains are decomposed, burned, mutilated or otherwise unrecognizable. After first ascertaining whether the remains are in fact human, the forensic anthropologist can then determine the gender, approximate age, physical stature and likely racial affiliation of the person in life. The examination can also yield approximate time since death, likely cause of death and any identifying illnesses or wounds suffered in life that could leave traces in the bone structure. However, while a forensic anthropologist may make recommendations as to the cause and manner of death, based on his or her interpretation of skeletal trauma, it is ultimately the medicolegal responsibility of the forensic pathologist to make the final determinations (Steadman 2003a, 127–37). It must be explained that forensic science is a coordinated team effort. Forensic anthropologists frequently team up with forensic pathologists, forensic dentists (odontologists), medical examiners, homicide detectives and DNA identification laboratories to identify the deceased as well as the time and manner of their death (Jurmain et al. 2007; Medicinenet.com 2008). Forensic anthropologists also utilize classic archaeological means of mapping, as well as ground surveys for the systematic recovery of buried remains and other artefacts of the burial. Information can also be gleaned by the analysis of pollen, soil, seeds and insects excavated from the site. Archaeological training allows these tell-tale forensic evidences to be recovered and properly documented.

Possible Forensic Applications

As earlier indicated, the following three case studies relate to skeletonized remains found in Trinidad and Tobago between 2006 and 2007, as described in media reports. The discussion will revolve around the various forensic anthropological methods considered most appropriate for these case studies.

First Case Study

Trinidad Guardian
Thursday, December 6, 2006, p. 22

Police Seek Help to Identify Body

Radhica Sookraj
Guardian South Bureau

Police are trying to identify the skeletal remains of a woman found on the San Fernando Hill on Tuesday. Detectives believe that the woman was about 25 years old and could have been dead for about four months. They said she was about five feet four inches tall with braids.

Officers have been checking on their missing persons files but have not yet found anyone matching the description of the deceased. Police are appealing to the public to report the names of any of their loved ones who have been missing for more than four months.

Forestry Division officers were cleaning bushes on the San Fernando Hill around 8 a.m. when they found the remains near Maryyat Street. The skeleton was taken to the Forensic Science Centre in Port-of-Spain.

Second Case Study

Trinidad Daily Express
Tuesday March 27, 2007, p. 9

Woman Stumbles Upon Human Bones

South Bureau

A woman working for an asphalt paving company stumbled onto the bones of a man in a cane field in the weekend. The discovery was made off the M2 Road, near Debe. The woman told police that about 3:15 p.m. on Saturday, she walked into the bushes near a quarry site, and found the bones.

A district medical officer told the police the bones belonged to an adult male and might have been at the site for a year. A red jersey was found near the remains. Southern Division police are checking their missing persons records. Southern Division Homicide is investigating.

Trinidad Daily Express
Thursday April 5, 2007

Tip-off Leads to Bones in Cane Field

Carolyn Kisson
South Bureau

An anonymous caller yesterday led the police to a cane field in Ste Madeleine, where they discovered a pile of human skeletal remains along with women's clothing. The bones were taken to the Forensic Science Centre in St James, where tests would be done to determine whether the remains are those of a woman or man.

Police said around 8:00 p.m. on Tuesday, they received a call that a body was dumped in a cane field at M2 Ring Road, Ste Madeleine. They went to the scene around 7 a.m. yesterday and found the bones. A dark coloured skirt, a strap blouse, red underwear and black bra were found near the remains, leading the investigators to believe that they were those of a woman. A police officer said the description of the clothing did not match any of their missing persons reports.

Officers attached to the Southern Division Homicide Bureau are continuing investigations.

In all three of these cases, remains are skeletonized, thereby making them appropriate for the skills and expertise of the forensic anthropologist. Also, the remains were all found outdoors. With respect to the first case study, the remains were discovered in San Fernando Hill, while in the second and third case studies, the victims were found in a cane field at M2 Ring Road near Debe (figure 2.1).

Both San Fernando Hill and the M2 Ring Road cane fields are relatively remote locations, with considerable plant growth, and apparently they were considered by assailants as ideal for concealing the bodies of their victims. Many murderers will go to great lengths to hide their dirty deeds by disposing of their victims in manners intended to avoid detection. Dismemberment and dispersal of body parts, burials, burning, submersion or stashing within walls, septic tanks, or under floors are

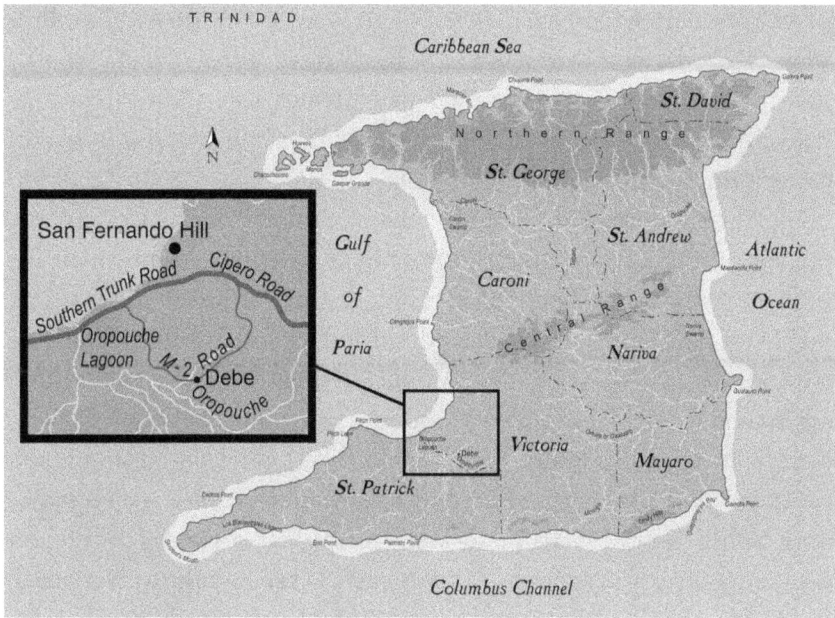

Figure 2.1
Approximate location of crime scenes in San Fernando Hill and at M2 Ring Road in southwestern Trinidad

just a few of the extremes to which perpetrators will go in order to conceal their crimes or to keep the body hidden close by to prolong their fantasies (Steadman 2003a). Thus, forensic anthropologists must know how to properly detect and recover decomposed bodies or skeletal remains from a variety of contexts. However, the most common context for which forensic anthropologists are consulted is the outdoor setting (ibid.).

Procedures in Forensic Anthropology

Determining whether the Bones Are Human

Clothes found at the scene of the crime in the second and third cases suggest that the remains are human. In the first case study, there is mention of a "woman about 25 years old about five feet four inches tall with braids". This suggests that, in addition to the remains not being entirely skeletonized, the deceased could be identified by some remaining soft tissue on the cranium and the presence of braids. However, differentiating between human and animal bones is not always easy. Generally, in cases for which there are several complete bones to examine (as described in the foregoing three case studies), distinguishing faunal from human bones is not much of an issue for the physical anthropologist. However, the presence of bones is often a problem for forensic pathologists and medical examiners who are not accustomed to dealing with either bones in isolation or those that may be fragmentary (Fairgrieve 1999b, 10–16).

The first question in any case is "are the remains human?" There are ways of distinguishing human from animal long bone fragments using defined radiographic characteristics and features (X-rays) (Chilvarquer et al. 1987). Genus and species identification is also possible using mitochondrial DNA (mtDNA) samples; although, this would require sacrificing a small sample of bone (Fairgrieve 1999b, 10–16). Identification also requires a comprehensive knowledge of the fauna within the general neighbourhood of the crime scene. Given its proximity to South America, Trinidad and Tobago has a continental fauna based on a diverse number of animals such as tapirs (tapirus terrestris), agoutis (dasyprocta leporina), capybaras (hydrochoerus hydrochaeris), pacas (cuniculus paca) and so on (Boomert 2000). Once such a list of suspected fauna is identified, the faunal skeletal reference collection must be consulted. These can be accessed through the Life Sciences Department of the University of the West Indies, St Augustine Campus, in Trinidad and Tobago. If the bones are positively identified as non-human rather than human, the investigation should be halted immediately as the case is no longer anthropological (see Fairgrieve 1999b, 10–16).

In a terrorist attack, human bones can commingle with animal bones, especially if there are many restaurants situated within residential or commercial districts. In the aftermath of the terrorist attack on the Twin Towers in New York City on September 11, 2001, which killed over two thousand people, physical anthropologists in New York were able to identify human remains that were in various conditions: burned, calcined, mummified and putrefied; these remains ranged from whole bodies to small bone fragments. Forensic anthropologists also solved some of the initial problems discerning human from nonhuman remains (Mundorff 2003). Several restaurants were located within the area of destruction and, therefore, it was expected that nonhuman remains would be collected during the excavation process (ibid.). While terrorism has yet to hit the Caribbean in its more dastardly and violent forms, such as the destruction of the World Trade Center Towers or the train bombings in London or Spain, the anglophone Caribbean has had two bouts of serious terrorism-type political violence, namely the 1983 Maurice Bishop coup in Grenada and the 1990 Muslimeen insurrection in Trinidad (Desoran 2007). The murder-suicide of more than nine hundred people in Jonestown, Guyana in June 1978 (Layton 1999) should also be a horrific reminder of what can happen in the region. These macabre events in the Caribbean serve to bring into sharp relief the ever-present need for forensic anthropologists to effectively deal with similar events in Trinidad and Tobago, and the wider Caribbean, should they arise in the future.

Search, Excavation and Recovery

Having established that the remains are in fact human, the forensic anthropologist is free to proceed with his or her investigations. Working with the skeletonized victims identified in the three case studies, the anthropologist would conduct an intense ground search for scattered remains and more clothing (see Love and Marks 2003). An appropriate search and recovery strategy must be developed based on the extent of the scatter and the local environmental conditions in which the remains were initially found. In the first case study, the San Fernando Hill, with its dense tree cover, would require ground surveys radiating from the primary site of decomposition. On the other hand, the cane fields of the M2 Ring Road, Ste Madeleine, could easily be trimmed to facilitate ground visibility and grids (of one- to five-metre intervals) set up in order to conduct a reconnaissance of areas in the vicinity of the skeletal discoveries. Searchers must remember that in the absence of bleaching, which turns the bones white, bones will become the colour of their surrounding matrix. For instance, if the soil colour is very dark, the bones will also become dark over time. Grass and certain metals, such as copper, will stain bones, providing clues about their original context if the remains had been scattered or purposefully moved (Steadman 2003a). Bullets and bullet casings found at the site should also be collected.

The primary site of decomposition would usually be of a different soil from the surrounding area because the former would have been affected by dead or yellowing vegetation caused by the highly acidic decomposition fluids. A soil sample would be taken from the decay site, by the forensic anthropologist, and a control site sample would be taken from nearby, but outside, the decay site. Perhaps the most exciting (and high-profile) recent application of both existing and new databases is within the field of soil forensics. Today there is general recognition that trace evidence (fibres, fluids and particles) found at a scene of crime can be instrumental in providing criminal intelligence to police investigations (Vector1Media 2008). Soil is a complex matrix composed of mineral grains, organic material, and living and decomposing organisms. The proportions and characteristics of the mineral, organic and biological components of soil vary, often in a unique manner. Soil particles readily adhere to, and transfer from clothing, shoes, vehicles or tools and can therefore be treated as trace evidence, potentially linking suspects to, or eliminating them from, a crime scene (ibid.). Research has shown that DNA evidence may be obtained from a small sample of soil recovered from the sole of a shoe and from soil stains on clothing, and therefore these samples could potentially be used as associative evidence to prove a link between suspects and crime scenes (Horswell et al. 2002). In Trinidad and Tobago, the stage is now set for DNA analysis, as the government recently announced that the DNA profiles of two thousand prisoners will form the core of a database being created under the DNA Act (Newsday 2008).

A proper excavation is critical, and one must have the correct tools for the job. Excavation of human remains is a delicate and time-consuming process. Trowels, brushes and wood picks can be used to fully expose the human remains (Steadman 2003a). The excavation of the skeletal remains at all three sites in Trinidad and Tobago should proceed by removing the soil in ten- to twenty-centimetre increments. Documentation of each step of the excavation is crucial. Photographs and maps are required and videotape may be used as well. It is vital that the forensic anthropologist keep meticulous excavation notes, including a description of the stratigraphic changes at each level and an inventory of the bones of the associated evidence observed. No evidence should be removed before the entire burial is exposed (ibid.). The depth of the burial, the position of the body (prone or supine, extended or flexed, for example) and the association of bones to other evidence, such as bullets, clothing or a wallet, should be documented in situ by photographs and maps (ibid.). Once the burial is fully exposed and documented, the bones and associated evidence may be removed and placed in labelled evidence bags. Biological materials, including bones, should be placed only in paper bags, as damp remains will mould if stored in plastic. Again, the floor of the burial should be excavated to look for additional evidence once the remains have been removed (ibid.).

Even in cases where the time span would be at the limits of what would be considered as "recent forensic interest" to the police, forensic anthropologists can expose significant evidence by employing archaeological mapping, documentation and photography. A notable example of this is the 1995 investigation of a homicide case that occurred in 1943 in the Danforth area of Toronto, Canada (Melbye et al. 1999). In the summer of 1995, workmen engaged in the demolition of Robertson Motors on Danforth Avenue, in Toronto, accidentally discovered human remains below an extensive, one-foot-thick cement pad that was being broken up by heavy machinery. Dr Jerry Melbye, a forensic anthropology consultant with the Chief Coroner's Office of Toronto, was called in to investigate the burial. It was immediately apparent from his initial observations that the backhoe had disturbed a major part of the burial. Infracranial human bones were scattered about the area; some bones had been piled up by well-meaning workmen. The skull and most of the bones of the torso were still in situ. Fragments of clothing and a pair of women's shoes were found in association with the human remains. The skull had been wrapped in a burlap bag, and a dental plate was visible in the mouth. No soft tissue was present, except a mass of head hair that was recovered between the burlap bag and the skull (ibid.).

In order to ascertain the identity of the deceased, Melbye and his team used surveying and excavation skills (characteristic of archaeology) in recovering evidence. First, he established a small local grid of one-metre squares over the burial and scattered remains. Upon obtaining a map of the entire construction area, Melbye was able to construct a large-scale map of the burial with a single datum point (figure 2.2).

All human bones and possible related artefacts were mapped from the disturbed area, photographed and bagged. The articulated bones in the grave area were cleaned of debris with trowel and brush. The skull of the deceased bore seven large wounds, which suggested that she was a victim of homicide. As a result of a battery of forensic tests relating to sex determination, race, age and stature, and peri-mortem pathology (such as the seven wounds in the skull) (figure 2.3), it was revealed that the unknown person, named "Dottie C" was a white female, aged between twenty-eight and forty, whose stature was between 5 feet 2 inches and 5 feet 8 inches (figure 2.4).

She was apparently the victim of a homicide sometime between 1940 and 1949 (Melbye et al. 1999). This case brings into sharp perspective

Figure 2.2
Map of burial
remains

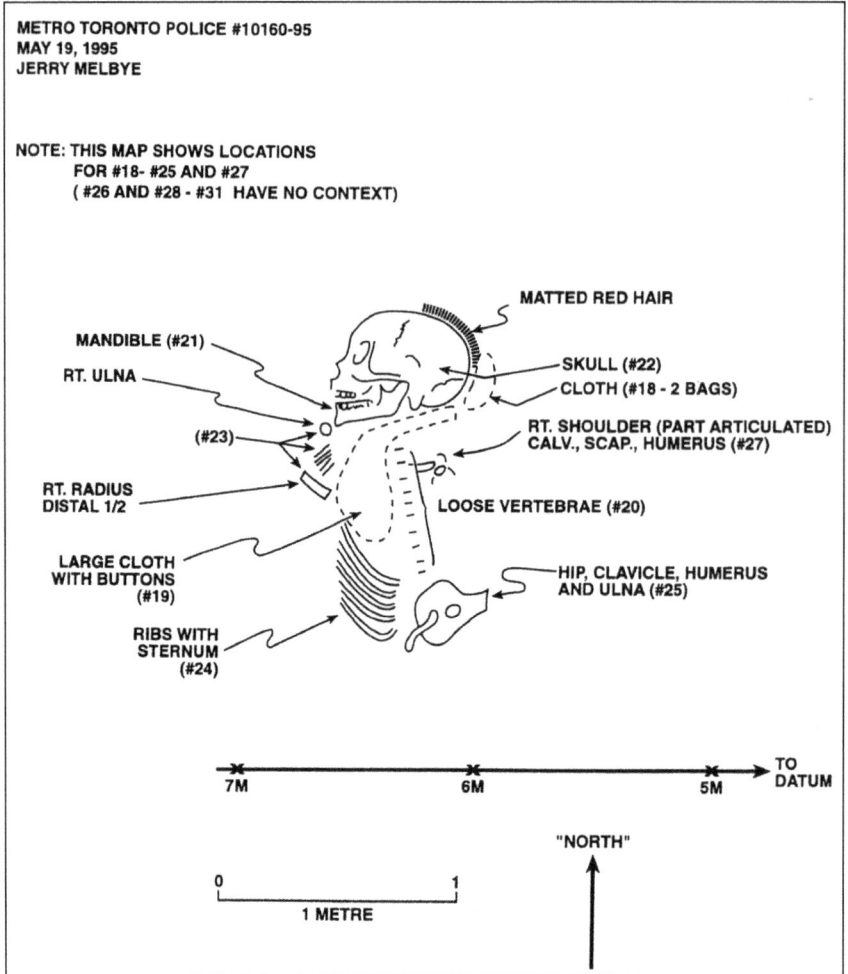

METRO TORONTO POLICE #10160-95
MAY 19, 1995
JERRY MELBYE

NOTE: THIS MAP SHOWS LOCATIONS
    FOR #18- #25 AND #27
    (#26 AND #28 - #31 HAVE NO CONTEXT)

MATTED RED HAIR

MANDIBLE (#21)

RT. ULNA

SKULL (#22)

CLOTH (#18 - 2 BAGS)

(#23)

RT. SHOULDER (PART ARTICULATED)
CALV., SCAP., HUMERUS (#27)

RT. RADIUS
DISTAL 1/2

LOOSE VERTEBRAE (#20)

LARGE CLOTH
WITH BUTTONS
(#19)

HIP, CLAVICLE, HUMERUS
AND ULNA (#25)

RIBS WITH
STERNUM
(#24)

7M   6M   5M

TO
DATUM

"NORTH"

0   1
1 METRE

Figure 2.3
Skull of "Dottie C",
showing wounds.
(Reproduced by
permission from
Fairgrieve 1999a,
97.)

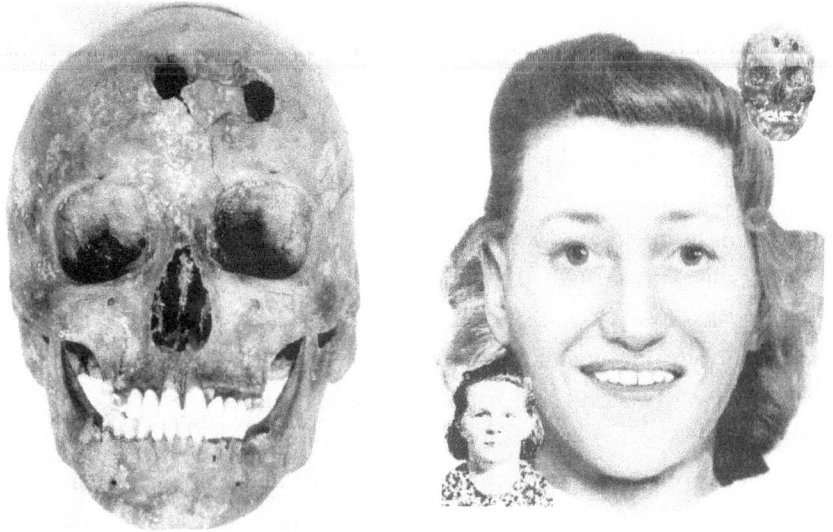

Figure 2.4
Facial reproduction
with insets of skull
and "Dottie C".
(Reproduced by
permission from
Fairgrieve 1999a,
104.)

the value of archaeological field techniques and how they can also be usefully applied in Trinidad and Tobago and the wider anglophone Caribbean.

Understanding the Importance of Context

It is vital that bones not be removed from the crime scene by law enforcement, medical examiners, coroners, and forensic pathologists, many of whom may erroneously feel that as the flesh decomposes the remains are somehow less human and/or have less forensic importance. Such misconceptions may lead to the violation of a number of protocols. For instance, every police investigator is trained not to disturb anything at a crime scene, especially the body, until the appropriate trained investigators arrive. However, it is not uncommon for forensic anthropologists in North America to arrive at a scene and find that the bones were picked up, examined and moved (Steadman 2003a). In the process, the context of the remains is compromised, which puts the anthropologist at an immediate disadvantage. Bones are also more portable than the entire body, and officials have been known to disturb a scene by picking up just one bone to take to the anthropologist so as to identify whether the bone is human. If the remains are human, then the anthropologist is working with a disturbed context. In general, forensic anthropologists would rather visit the scene than have the scene brought to them piece by piece (ibid.). In Trinidad and Tobago and the wider anglophone Caribbean, human skeletal remains are usually studied and processed by forensic pathologists, very often with little or no training in the basic techniques of forensic anthropology.

Interpreting Time since Death

Estimating time since death is a difficult aspect of the death scene investigation (Love and Marks 2003). Immediately after death, the body cools, developing varying degrees of rigour mortis, and then it undergoes tissue decay that culminates in skeletonization (Ubelaker 1999). The rates of these processes, especially tissue decay, are dramatically affected by diverse environmental conditions. If the corpse was buried, rate of decay is influenced by soil activity, groundwater retention and type of container. If exposed above the ground, decomposition is hastened by foraging mammals, birds and insects. All variables differ by environment, season and method of treatment of the body. In a hot and humid climate, with exposure to scavengers, a body can become skeletonized in two weeks. By contrast, in extremely dry regions such as the desert coasts of Chile and Peru, desiccated soft tissue can be preserved for thousands of years (Ubelaker 1999). Additional clues may come from the state of preservation of associated materials. Morse and Daily (1985) presented experimental data on rates of decomposition of various types of clothing and other grave goods under different conditions. Rayon disintegrated most rapidly. Other materials tested showed the following order of increasing resistance to decomposition: paper, untreated cotton, treated cotton, silk, wool, human hair, polyester, triacetate, nylon, leather, plastic and acrylic (Ubelaker 1999). Willey and Heilman (1987) argued that it is possible for plants to provide clues about time since death. In their view, the stems and woody roots of perennial trees have annual growth rings, which can be counted to establish the age of a plant growing through clothing or having some other relationship with the body. In temperate countries, perennial trees tend to grow and bloom over the spring and summer and then die every winter, growing back in the spring from their root stock rather than seeding themselves as an annual tree does. This method therefore has limited usefulness for Trinidad and Tobago and the wider Caribbean, given the lack of such well-defined seasons in the region.

Both forensic pathologists and forensic anthropologists are called upon to estimate the time between death and discovery. In order to accurately evaluate a decomposing body they often turn to the research of various disciplines, including entomology (Love and Marks 2003). Forensic entomology, which is the study of insects associated with a body after death, can determine time since death. The first insects to colonize a body are usually the Calliphoridae, or blow fly. They will lay their eggs on the corpse, usually in a wound or in any of the natural orifices. Knowledge of their developmental stages can provide an approximate time of death (Anderson 1995). In the first case study, investigators surmised that the deceased found in the San Fernando Hill may have been dead for about four months; in the second case, the remains were allegedly at the site for a year, while no timeline was given in the third case. It is unclear as to what benchmarks were used by investigators to determine the time since death in the first and second cases. The four-month timeline for the San Fernando remains seems arbitrary, given the hot, humid climate of Trinidad and Tobago with its abundance of foraging creatures. Given local conditions in the twin island republic, human bodies left outdoors would usually be skeletonized within two to three weeks. The one-year timeline estimated in the second case study suggests that the skeletal remains found at the cane fields of the M2 Ring Road, Ste Madeleine, bear less soft tissue, although only a forensic anthropologist could provide a more definitive answer on the timeline between death and discovery.

Equipped with a unique open-air research laboratory designed exclusively for longitudinally studying decomposition in East Tennessee, William Bass and coworkers at the University of Tennessee have analysed hundreds of bodies progressing through various stages of decomposition, and documented the post-mortem interval at each stage (Love and Marks 2003). Only two phases will be mentioned here, given their relevance to this chapter:

Phase 1. *Skeletonization:* Bloating completely subsided; soft tissue continues to deteriorate.

Phase 2. *Skeleton decomposition:* All soft tissue consumed; skeleton completely disarticulated; cortex of bone begins to crack and age.

The early phase of skeletonization seems to be more pertinent to the first case study in San Fernando Hill, as some soft tissue was still intact, at least on the cranium. Not enough information was provided in the media reports on the second and third cases to accurately determine whether they relate to the more advanced skeleton decomposition phase, as described by William Bass. On all counts, it would be difficult to provide timelines for all three cases unless a forensic anthropologist provided a detailed analysis of the remains.

Laboratory Analysis

Having completed the skeletal and evidence recovery from San Fernando Hill and the M2 Ring Road cane fields, the forensic anthropologist would return with the materials to the forensic laboratory to begin the analysis. The skeletal remains relating to the first case study from the San Fernando Hill should be processed to remove the remaining soft tissue to assess trauma, age and sex (see Love and Marks 2003). The first phase of the analysis begins with a skeletal inventory of the presence or absence of each element, as well as any duplication of elements that might be present (indicating that there is more than one individual represented). Placing the remains in anatomical order also facilitates the completion of the skeletal inventory, which is critical to documenting and maintaining the proper sequencing of bones (Simmons and Haglund 2005). The inventory must also note the condition of the remains at this stage of the analysis, including a taphonomic assessment of post-mortem damage (examples include staining, carnivore and rodent gnawing, breakage, weathering, root etching, and so on). The condition of each element should be noted. It is recommended that the anthropologist prepare, in advance, a list of post-mortem damage likely to be seen in forensic cases (ibid.).

(1) Establishing the Biological Profile of the Deceased

Creating a basic biological profile of the deceased is an integral part of forensic analysis, as this helps to positively identify the individual. Determining biological sex, ancestry, age and stature during life are key aspects of biological profiles. Biological sex (not gender) must be assessed first, as it will prescribe the methods used for the estimation for both age and stature. When a forensic anthropologist examines a skeleton, he or she is determining the individual's sex, not his or her gender. Sex is a biological consequence of chromosomal inheritance; gender is a social construct based on how the individual self-identified, was classified by his or her culture, and behaved during life. While gender may be inferred from the context in which the skeleton appears (clothing, personal effects and so on), the anthropologist needs to assess the skeleton independently of these features first to determine biological sex (Simmons and Haglund 2005).

In the second Trinidad and Tobago case study, a red jersey was found near the remains, while in the third case study a dark-coloured skirt, a strap blouse, red underwear and black bra were found near the remains. Clothing suggests male and female genders respectively but not necessarily the biological sexes of the victims. The forensic anthropologist would determine the biological sexes of the Trinidad and Tobago skeletons based largely on discrete differences in size and shape between the male and female pelvis that reflect structural differences arising from the female's childbearing capabilities. While the male exhibits a narrow, heart-shaped pelvic inlet, the female pelvis is comparatively wider and elliptically shaped. While the female sciatic notch

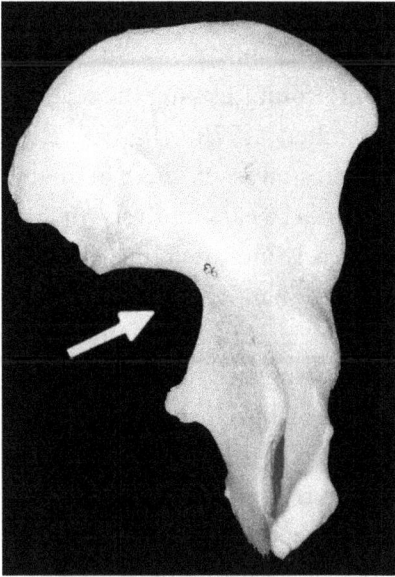

Figure 2.5 Female sciatic notch.
(Reproduced by permission from Fairgrieve 1999a, 23.)

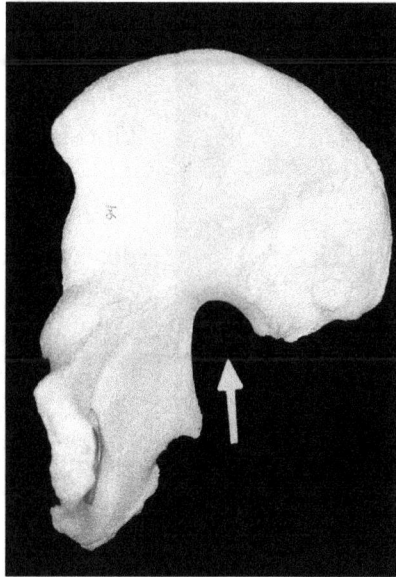

Figure 2.6 Male sciatic notch.
(Reproduced by permission from Fairgrieve 1999a, 24.)

in the pelvis is wider, the male's sciatic notch is narrower (figures 2.5 and 2.6).

In general, male skulls tend to be larger and more robust that their female counterparts. The male face exhibits prominent supraorbital ridges and glabellar region, blunt edges on the eye orbits, and a large mastoid process. However, the female face presents a relatively smoother glabellar region and small to medium supraorbital ridge (figure 2.7) (Walsh-Henry et al. 1999).

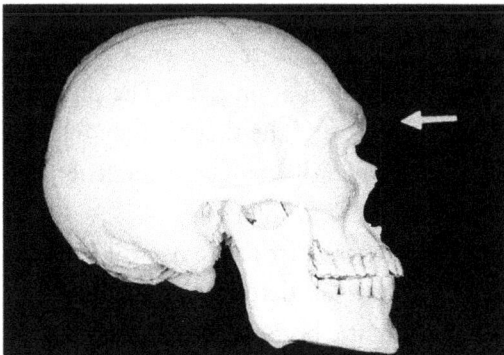

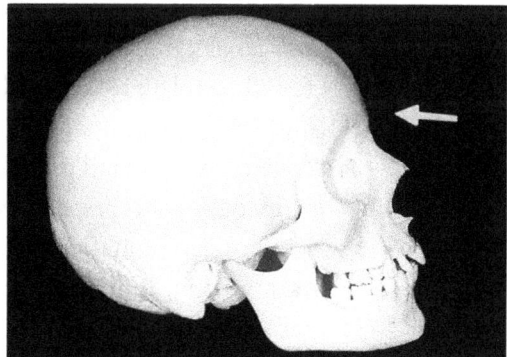

Figure 2.7 Male skull (left): arrow indicates presence of well-developed supraorbital ridge and glabellar region; female skull (right): arrow indicates the more vertical forehead and relatively flat supraorbital ridge. (Reproduced by permission from Fairgrieve 1999a, 26.)

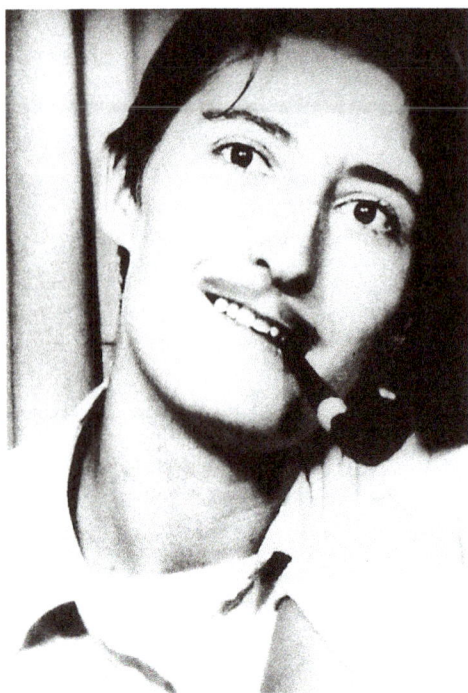

Figure 2.8
Photograph taken during life of the misidentified female. (Reproduced by permission from Fairgrieve 1999a, 30.)

These criteria were effectively used in establishing the identity of a misidentified female whose remains were found by investigators in Florida in September 1978 (figure 2.8). Although the skeleton was clothed in men's pants, shirt and underwear, analysis of the deceased skeleton clearly indicated that the individual was in fact a woman who was known to dress as a male. Investigators eventually found the perpetrators who confessed to murdering the victim in her home and burying the body near her home (Walsh-Henry et al. 1999).

Other components of the deceased biological profile are age, stature and race. The appearance and union of centres of bone growth, and certain other changes in bones and teeth, help the investigator in determining the age of the individual at the time of death. For example, young adults and older adults have several methods of age determination: closure of the cranial sutures; morphology of rib-ends, auricular surface and pubic symphysial; microstructure of bone and teeth and wear on teeth (Age Determination n.d.). Cranial sutures (non-movable joints in the head) slowly fuse together, becoming obliterated in time. Although this has been known for many years, there has only been a weak association established between age and closure. The morphology of rib-ends changes over time. Ribs are connected to the sternum by cartilage. The rib ends that meet with the cartilage are relatively flat at first, but during the aging process the ends become ragged and the cartilage becomes pitted. The irregularity of the rib ends has been found to relate to age at death (Age Determination n.d.). The physical anthropologist can also calculate the stature of the skeletal remains discovered in Trinidad and Tobago by applying formulae to the length of individual bones, especially the long bones of limbs.

Race determination is viewed as a critical part of the overall identification of an individual's remains. However, determining ancestry or race from skeletons can be very problematic because there are no generally agreed upon criteria to define racial groups in humans, the nature of variation within and between populations, and the effects of interbreeding among human populations (Pietrusewsky n.d.). Unlike

Jamaica, where over 90 per cent of the population is of African descent (Satchell 1999), Trinidad and Tobago has a marked ethnic plurality, reflective of the country's history of conquest and immigration. Of the twin island republic's 1.3 million inhabitants, approximately 96 per cent reside on the island of Trinidad with the remaining 4 per cent in Tobago. According to the 2000 census, Trinidad's ethnic composition is as follows: East Indian 40.0 per cent, African 37.5 per cent, mixed 20.5 per cent, European 0.6 per cent, Chinese 0.3 per cent, other or not stated 1.1 per cent (Bureau of Western Hemisphere Affairs 2008). Euro-Trinidadians, especially those descendants of the former plantocracy, are often referred to as French Creoles, even if they are descended from Spanish, British or German settlers. The Cocoa Panyols are descendants of the original Spanish settlers and later immigrants from Venezuela (Saunders 2005). Today, the Trinidadian Portuguese population includes both whites and mixed people. The small Amerindian population, primarily comprised of Carib descendants, are primarily organized around the Santa Rosa Carib Community, based in Arima (Forte 2005). Some forensic anthropologists in North America substitute the terms "ancestry" or "ethnic group" to avoid reference to a possible typological race concept (Ubelaker 2004). Kennedy (1995) has discussed the line walked by forensic anthropologists in this area of study and the complexity he himself has experienced teaching both forensic anthropology and the dynamics of human variation at the university level. Sauer (1992, 1993) and Ubelaker (1996) have argued that in estimating "racial affiliation" for law enforcement (in the United States, for example), most forensic anthropologists do not utilize a Blumenbach-like classification of world populations but rather attempt to determine how persons would have been regarded by the communities within which they lived.

In North America, forensic anthropologists generally use a three-race model to categorize skeletal traits: Caucasian (European), Asian (Asian and Amerindian) and African (African and West Indian). Although there are certainly some common physical characteristics among these groups, not all individuals have skeletal traits that are completely consistent with their geographic origin. Second, people of mixed racial ancestry are common. The mention of braids, on the skeletonized remains of the deceased in San Fernando Hill in the first case study, suggests that the victim may have been of African descent, but a much more comprehensive examination of the remains would be

Table 2.1: Determination of Race from Skull

Diagnostic Features	Southwestern Native American of Asian Ancestry	Americans of European Ancestry	Americans of African Ancestry
Overall shape	Short base chord; base angle high; keeled skull (bump at top)	Long base chord; base angle low	Long base chord (longest); base angle low (lowest); post-bregmatic depression
Shape of nasals	Tented nasals (narrower than African American); nasal overgrowth; nasal opening flared at base; blurred nasal sill	Tower nasals (steep); large nasal spine; sharp nasal sill; depressed nasion (under glabella)	Nasal opening flared; small nasal spine; guttered nasal sill
Ascending ramus	Wide ascending ramus	Most pinched ascending ramus	Less pinched ascending ramus
Chin	Vertical chin; blunt chin	Prominent chin; bilobate chin	Vertical chin; blunt chin
Teeth	Shovel-shaped teeth	Carabelli's cusp (accessory cusp on maxillary molar)	Molar crenulations (folded appearance, esp. 2nd and 3rd)

required to more definitively determine the genetic ancestry of the deceased. Despite the many drawbacks associated with ethnic ancestral identifications, there are still some fundamental differences in the morphology of human skulls that can be used in differentiating between certain racial groups (Kennedy 1995). Table 2.1 presents some differences (Marci's Anthro Page 2006).

In North America, forensic anthropologists frequently use FORDISC 2.0, a computer programme, to assist in the identification of unknown skeletonized individuals. Developed by Steven Ousley and Richard Jantz at the University of Tennessee (Ousley and Jantz 1996), this programme is capable of performing two primary functions. Using standard cranial and postcranial measurements, it can classify unknown individuals into ancestry and sex groups by using multiple discriminant function analyses, and it can also derive stature estimations by least-squares regression methods (Sanders 2002). However, FORDISC is based on the United States Forensic Database, where ancestry, age distribution and socio-economic status (based on population samples) may differ significantly from those of the anglophone Caribbean, thereby limiting its usefulness for our region. Ramsthaler et al. (2007) argued that the use of FORDISC as a single method for the estimation of biological sex of recent skeletal remains even in Europe cannot be recommended without additional morphological assessment and without a built-in software update based on modern European population samples. In charting the way forward, forensic experts in the Caribbean should explore the possibility of devising a forensic computer programme that is more accurately reflective of the age distributions, stature, ethnic ancestries and socio-economic classifications of the region.

According to Lotter (2008), DNA technologies have enormous forensic implications in the fight against crime, especially mitochondrial DNA (mtDNA). MtDNA, found in bones, teeth and hair shafts, can be used to identify crime and catastrophe victims (Human Genome Project Information 2008). This was the case in the aftermath of the World Trade Center disaster. Because the nuclear DNA (nDNA) found in bone evidence is frequently limited and/or degraded, mtDNA analysis is often the analysis method of choice (Forensic Science Communications 2005). The skeletal remains found in the three Trinidad and Tobago case studies, as well as the hair of the victim found in the San Fernando Hill, would be ideal samples for mtDNA analysis. The identity of individuals could therefore be established, provided that the "missing persons" databases in Trinidad and Tobago and the rest of the anglophone Caribbean are sufficiently comprehensive and up-to-date. The antemortem X-rays of the teeth can be compared with the teeth of the deceased in order to establish the victim's identity.

(2) Determining Cause and Manner of Death

Media reports on the physical characteristics of human skeletons found at the San Fernando Hill and the M2 Ring Road in St Madeleine are limited; hence, it is impossible to determine the cause and manner of death of the victims. However, a forensic anthropologist, upon studying the remains, would be able to provide some useful insights. A fractured hyoid bone may suggest death by strangulation (figure 2.9) (Goodman and Himmelberger 2002).

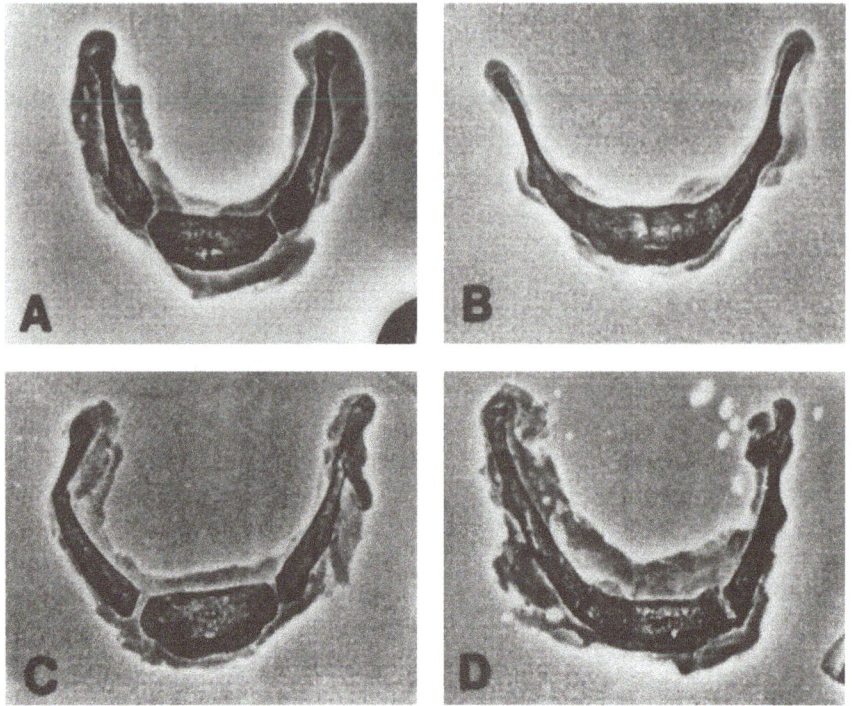

Figure 2.9
Fractured and unfractured hyoid bones: (a) unfused and unfractured hyoid bone; (b) fused and unfractured hyoid bone; (c) unfused and symmetrically fractured hyoid bone in manual strangulation; (d) fused and fractured hyoid bone in manual strangulation. (Reproduced by permission from Fairgrieve 1999a, 191.)

Club blows produce dents with cracks radiating from them, knives produce narrow cuts, machetes produce longitudinal fractures (figure 2.10) while spears and other piecing weapons produce well-defined holes.

If there are entrance and exit bullet wounds on the skeleton, particularly the skull, the physical anthropologist can make a significant contribution to death investigations by examining fracture patterns and the bevelling of entrance and exit wounds to determine the direction of fire (for example, front to back or left to right) and the minimum number of bullets that impacted a skeleton (Steadman 2003b). For example, radiographs of the fragmented skull of the misidentified female found in Florida in 1978 showed numerous shotgun pellets and lead streaks. It was therefore concluded that the victim was shot behind the ear, with the shotgun blast entering on the lower margin of the right parietal, leaving an entrance wound that was irregular in shape (Walsh-Henry et al. 1999).

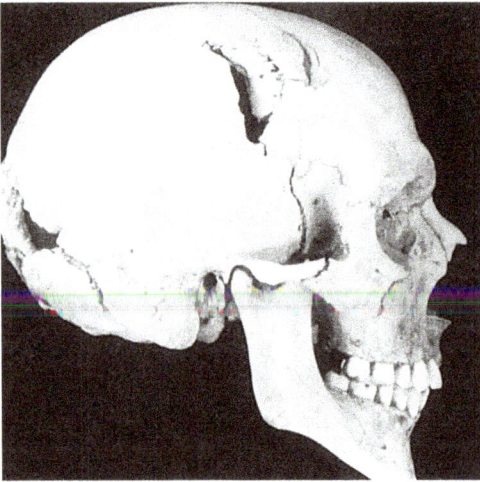

Figure 2.10
Skull showing multiple fractures from a tool. (Reproduced by permission from Maples and Browning 1994, 116–17.

The highly publicized 1981 La Belle Drug Murder Case is another example of forensic anthropologists being able to determine cause and manner of death by examining human skeletons (Maples and Browning 1994). According to an informant, who was a key witness in the court case, three businessmen came down from the northeastern United States to Florida to negotiate with some local drug smugglers. As often happens in these sordid cases, negotiations broke down. The three businessmen were kidnapped from their hotel in Fort Myers and eventually shot and buried. In 1984, Dr William Maples and Brenda Sigler-Eisenberg, both attached to the University of Florida in Gainesville, spearheaded the excavation of these human remains. As the pit was slowly excavated, what was exposed was most revealing (figure 2.11).

The uppermost body was that of a man whose hands were tied tightly behind his back. His body was arched like a bow, since the other end of the rope was tied to his ankles. His head was encircled with duct tape and showed clear evidence of a shotgun wound from a gun fired at close range. During the excavation, the archaeologists found small plastic wrappers that had encircled buckshot in shotgun shells. By the location of these wrappers, on the top of the bodies between them, Sigler-Eisenberg and Maples were able to establish the sequence of

Figure 2.11
The three excavated bodies in the La Belle murder pit. (Reproduced by permission from Maples and Browning 1994, 116–17.)

events. The body buried deepest had been shot last, not first. Their conclusion was later corroborated by the informant who testified in court that the man who laid bottommost in the grave was actually the last to die. After the men were kidnapped from the hotel, they realized that their situation was hopeless. Contemplating his fate, knowing that there was no escape, the third man had begged to be executed first, so that he would not have to watch the other two murders. In an exquisite refinement of cruelty, his tormentors threw him in the pit face down, alive, shot his colleagues so they would fall on him, and only then did they shoot him through the "V" of his open-necked shirt. As a result of the La Belle excavation, whose results were reinforced by the informant's testimony in court, close to twenty people went to jail for various offences relating to drug trafficking and murder (Maples and Browning 1994).

The La Belle drug murder case should have considerable applicability for Trinidad and Tobago and the wider Caribbean, given the frequency of drug-related murders in the region (Economist.com 2008). Toxicology reports from homicide victims in Trinidad and Tobago indicate that a significant proportion of homicides are directly or indirectly linked to drug use and dealing, suggesting that "drug-related" homicide may be currently underestimated in the twin island republic (Maguire and Kuhns 2006). Further, police departments in Trinidad and Tobago, like elsewhere in the Caribbean, often mischaracterize homicide motive by ignoring potential drug use or drug-dealing linkages. Griffith (1997) has provided a comprehensive study of the drug dilemma in the Caribbean that reveals the severity of the threat illegal drug trafficking poses to the small countries of that region. The increase in the production and flow of drugs undermines the political stability and economic development because it leads to crime, corruption and arms trafficking (ibid.).

Conclusions

The foregoing discussion places a much-needed spotlight on the usefulness of forensic anthropology for the region, based on three case studies drawn from Trinidad and Tobago. Jamaica, Guyana and Trinidad and Tobago, for example, continue to witness alarming homicide rates, with the victims of crimes often becoming skeletonized. There have been several incidents throughout the anglophone Caribbean of human bodies being mutilated, burned beyond recognition or completely disarticulated (Jamaica Newsweekly 2006; Westindiantimes.net 2006; *Newsday* 2007). These cases are all tailor-made for the skills and expertise of forensic anthropologists.

Fortunately, a forensic science infrastructure already exists in the region. As earlier indicated, there are a number of forensic science centres and units scattered throughout the English-speaking Caribbean, in countries such as Trinidad and Tobago, Jamaica, Barbados, and the Bahamas. The University of the West Indies, which has its three main campuses in Trinidad and Tobago, Jamaica, and Barbados, has forensic pathology units located within the university's medical faculties. In September 2009, the Basic Medicine Department of University of the West Indies at Mona, Jamaica, will offer a master's degree in forensic science, of which forensic anthropology is a part (Wayne McClaughlin, personal communication, 2007).

However, those who may not wish to pursue forensic anthropology as part of a medical degree are required to study at considerable expense in overseas universities, such as the University of Florida, the University of Tennessee, the University of London and Southampton University. Caribbean governments should therefore offer scholarships to young forensic aspirants, based on the premise that upon completing their course of study overseas, they will be bonded to work for a specified period within the region. In the United States, there are fewer than one hundred forensic anthropologists certified as diplomates of the American Board of Forensic Anthropology. Of this number, there are only about fifty who are currently active in the field. Most diplomates work in the academic field and consult on casework as it arises. The anglophone Caribbean region, given its size, could therefore be comfortably serviced by about five forensic anthropologists who would work closely with law enforcement officials. CARICOM decided to take joint action against murders, kidnappings, drug trafficking and violent gangs in the region by signing a Maritime and Airspace and Security Agreement in June 2008. Perhaps CARICOM should also consider funding persons who have expressed an interest in pursuing careers in forensic anthropology, as having a cadre of forensic anthropologists in the anglophone Caribbean would undoubtedly be a major fillip to our ongoing crime-fighting efforts.

References

Adamson, Marci. 2006. Determination of Race from Skull. *Marci's Anthro Page*. http://www.anthrogirl.com/anthropage/raceskull.htm (accessed February 11, 2008).

Anderson, G.S. 1995. The Use of Insects in Death Investigations: An Analysis of Cases in British Columbia over a Five Year Period. *Canadian Society of Forensic Sciences Journal* 28 (4): 277–92.

Boomert, Arie. 2000. *Trinidad, Tobago and the Lower Orinoco Sphere: An Archaeological and Ethnohistorical Study*. Alkmaar, Netherlands: Cairi.

Brickely, Megan, and Roxane Ferlini, eds. 2007. *Forensic Anthropology: Case Studies from Europe*. Springfield, IL: Charles C. Thomas.

Bureau of Western Hemisphere Affairs. 2008. Background Note: Trinidad and Tobago. http://www.state.gov/r/pa/ei/bgn/35638.htm (accessed July 10, 2008).

Chilvarquer, I., D.M. Glassman, T.J. Prihoda and J.A. Cottone. 1987. Comparative Radiographic Study of Human and Animal Long Bones. *Journal of Forensic Sciences* 32 (6): 1645–54.

Desoran, Ramesh, ed. 2007. *Crime, Delinquency and Justice: A Caribbean Reader*. Kingston: Ian Randle.

Douglas, Luke. 2007. UWI to Offer First Degree in Forensic Science. *Jamaica Observer*. January 28. http://www.jamaicaobserver.com/news/html/20070127T180000-0500_118402_OBS_UWI_TO_OFFER_FIRST_DEGREE_IN_FORENSIC_SCIENCE_.asp (accessed February 21, 2008).

Economist. 2008. Murder in the Caribbean. Economist.com. January 31. http://www.economist.com/world/la/displaystory.cfm?story_id=10609414 (accessed February 6, 2008).

Fairgrieve, Scott, ed. 1999a. *Forensic Osteological Analysis: A Book of Case Studies*. Springfield, IL: Charles C. Thomas.

———. 1999b. Of Beasts and Humans: A Case of Recognition. In *Forensic Osteological Analysis: A Book of Case Studies*, ed. Scott Fairgrieve, 10–16. Springfield, IL: Charles C. Thomas.

Federal Bureau of Investigations. 2005. Interlaboratory Study on Bone Extraction for Mitochondrial DNA Analysis. *Forensic Science Communications* 7 (2). http://www.fbi.gov/hq/lab/fsc/backissu/april2005/communications/2005_04_communications02.htm (accessed February 10, 2008).

Fisher, Russell S. 1993. History of Forensic Pathology and Related Laboratory Sciences. In *Spitz and Fisher's Medicolegal Investigation of Death: Guidelines for the Application of Pathology to Crime Investigation*, ed. Werner U. Spitz, 3–13. Springfield, IL: Charles C. Thomas.

Forte, Maximillan C. 2005. *Ruins of Absence, Presence of Caribs: (Post) Colonial Representations of Aboriginality in Trinidad and Tobago*. Gainesville: University Press of Florida.

Frater, Adrian. 2008. Skeletal Remains Found in Hanover: Believed to Be Those of Missing Children. *Jamaica Gleaner*. February 7. http://www

.jamaica-gleaner.com/gleaner/20080207/lead/lead2.html (accessedFebruary 7, 2008).

Goodman, Norman R., and Linda K. Himmelberger. 2002. Identifying Skeletal Remains Found in a Sewer. *Journal of the American Dental Association* 133 (11): 1508–13. http://jada.ada.org/cgi/content/full/133/11/1508 (accessed February 10, 2008).

Griffith, Ivelaw Lloyd. 1997. *Drugs and Security in the Caribbean: Sovereignty Under Siege*. Philadelphia: Penn State Press.

Horswell, J., S.J. Cordiner, E.W. Maas, T.M. Martin, B.W. Sutherland, T.W. Speir and B. Nogales. 2002. Forensic Comparison of Soils by Bacterial Community DNA Profiling. *Journal of Forensic Sciences* 47 (2). http://www.astm.org/cgi-bin/SoftCart.exe/JOURNALS/FORENSIC/ PAGES/JFS4720350.htm?E+mystore (accessed February 10, 2008).

Hunter, John, and Margaret Cox. 2005. *Forensic Archaeology: Advances in Theory and Practice*. London: Routledge.

Jamaica Newsweekly. 2006. *Jamaica Newsletter Service*. February 26. http://www.jamaicans.com/news/weeknews/jamaica-newsweekly-for-th-113.shtml (accessed February 6, 2008).

———. 2007. *Jamaica Newsletter Service*. January 19. http://www.jamaicans. com/news/weeknews/jamaica-newsweekly-for-th-160.shtml (accessed February 6, 2008).

Jurmain, Robert, Lynn Kilgore Robert and Wenda Trevanthan. 2007. *Introduction to Physical Anthropology*. Belmont, CA: Thomson Wadsworth.

Khan, Sharief. 2008. Eleven Shot in Guyana Village Massacre. *Vancouver Sun*. January 26. http://www.canada.com/vancouversun/news/story.html?id= 0c5c18ef-6bd0-444e-9045-9ba828041bb8&k=67712 (accessed February 6, 2008).

Kennedy, K.A.R. 1995. But Professor, Why Teach Race Identification If Race Does not Exist? *Journal of Forensic Science* 40 (5): 779–800.

Layton, Deborah. 1999. *Seductive Poison: A Jonetown Survivor's Story of Life and Death in the People's Temple*. New York: Anchor.

Liem, M.C.A., and F. Koenraadt. 2007. Homicide-Suicide in the Netherlands: A Study of Newspaper Reports, 1992–2005. *Journal of Forensic Psychiatry and Psychology* 18 (4): 482–93.

Lotter, Karen. 2008. What Is Mitochondrial DNA? Suite101.com. January 6. http://forensicscience.suite101.com/article.cfm/what_is_mitochond rial_dna (accessed February 10, 2008).

Love, Jennifer C., and Murray K. Marks. 2003. Taphonomy and Time: Estimating the Postmortem Interval. In *Hard Evidence: Case Studies in Forensic Anthropology*, ed. Dawnie Wolfe Steadman, 160–75. New York: Prentice Hall.

Maguire, E., and J. Kuhns. 2006. Drug-Related Homicides in Trinidad and Tobago. Paper presented at the annual meeting of the American Society of Criminology (ASC). http://www.allacademic.com/meta/p127396_index. html (accessed February 9, 2008).

Maples, William R., and Michael Browning. 1994. *Dead Men Do Tell Tales: The Strange and Fascinating Cases of a Forensic Anthropologist*. New York: Doubleday.

Medicinenet.com. 2008. Definition of Forensic Anthropology. http://www .medterms.com/script/main/art.asp?articlekey=23310 (accessed January 23, 2008).

Melbye, Jerry, David Chiasson, Robert Wood and Barry Blenkinsop. 1999. Death on the Danforth. In *Forensic Osteological Analysis: A Book of Case Studies*, ed. Scott Fairgrieve, 89–106. Springfield, IL: Charles C. Thomas.

Minnesota State University. 2007. Age Determination. Minnesota State University EMuseum. http://www.mnsu.edu/emuseum/biology/forensics /age_determ.html (accessed February 10, 2008).

Morse, Dan, and Robert C. Daily. 1985. The Degree of Deterioration of Associated Death Scene Material. *Journal of Forensic Sciences* 30 (1): 119–27.

Mundorff, Amy Zelson. 2003. Urban Anthropology: Case Study from New York City Medical Examiner's Office. In *Hard Evidence: Case Studies in Forensic Anthropology*, ed. Dawnie Wolfe Steadman, 52–62. Upper Saddle River, NJ: Prentice Hall.

Newsday. 2008. 2,000 "Cons" for DNA Database. February 9.

———. 2007. Pensioner Dies in Maracas Fire. December 12. http://www.news day.co.tt/crime_and_court/0,69638.html (accessed February 6, 2008).

Ousely, S., and R. Jantz. 1996. Fordisc 2.0. Knoxville: University of Tennessee.

Pietrusewsky, M. N.d. Ancestry/Race Determination, Forensic Anthropology, Lab. #3. http://www.anthropology.hawaii.edu/courses/anth458/images/ ancestry.pdf (accessed July 10, 2008).

Ramsthaler, F., K. Kreutz and M.A. Verhoff. 2007. Accuracy of Metric Sex Analysis of Skeletal Remains using Fordisc® Based on a Recent Skull Collection. *International Journal of Legal Medicine* 121 (6): 477–82. http://www.springerlink.com/content/2108815035411064/ (accessed February 10, 2008).

Reichs, Kathleen J. 1998. *Forensic Osteology: Advances in the Identification of Human Remains*. 2nd ed. Springfield, IL: Charles C. Thomas.

Sanders, Jason. 2002. A Test of the Postcranial Discriminant Functions of FORDISC 2.0 using the Hamann-Todd Collection. MSc. thesis. University of Indianapolis, Indiana. http://archlab.uindy.edu/documents/theses/ SandersJLAbstract.pdf (accessed February 10, 2008).

Satchell, Veront. 1999. Jamaica. http://www.hartford-hwp.com/archives/ 43/130.html (accessed July 10, 2008).

Sauer, N.J. 1992. Forensic Anthropology and the Concept of Race: If Races Don't Exist, Why Are Forensic Anthropologists so Good at Identifying Them? *Social Science of Medicine* 34 (2): 107–11.

———. 1993. Applied Anthropology and the Concept of Race: A Legacy of Linneaus. In *Race, Ethnicity and Applied Bioanthropology*, ed. C.C. Gordon, 79–84. National Association for the Practice of Anthropology Bulletin, no. 13 (Arlington: American Anthropological Association).

Saunders, Nicholas J. 2005. *The Peoples of the Caribbean: An Encyclopedia of Archaeology and Traditional Culture.* Santa Barbara, CA: ABC-CLIO.

Simmons, Tal, and William D. Haglund. 2005. Anthropology in a Forensic Legal Context. In *Forensic Archaeology: Advances in Theory and Practice,* ed. John Hunter and Margaret Cox, 157–75. London: Routledge.

Steadman, Dawnie Wolfe. 2003a. *Hard Evidence: Case Studies in Forensic Anthropology.* Upper Saddle River, NJ: Prentice Hall.

———. 2003b Interpretation of Trauma and Taphonomy. In *Hard Evidence: Case Studies in Forensic Anthropology,* ed. Dawnie Wolfe Steadman, 127–37. Upper Saddle River, NJ: Prentice Hall.

Stover, E., and M. Ryan. 2001. Breaking Bread With the Dead. *Historical Archeology* 32 (1): 7–25.

Trinidad Daily Express. 2007. Bones of Missing Mom Found. June 21, 9.

Trinidad Guardian. 2006. Dental Analysis to Identify Burnt Bodies. December, 8, 21.

Ubelaker, Douglas H. 1996. Skeletons Testify: Anthropology in Forensic Science. *Yearbook of Physical Anthropology* 39: 229–44.

———. 1999. *Human Skeletal Remains: Excavation, Analysis, and Interpretation.* Third Edition. Washington, DC: Smithsonian Institution.

———. 2004. Physical Anthropology: The Question of Race and Physical Variation. In *Race and Research Perspectives on Minority Participation in Health Studies,* ed. Bettine M. Beech and Maurine Goodman, 27–33. Washington, DC: American Public Heath Association.

US Department of Energy Office of Science, Office of Biological and Environmental Research, Human Genome Program. 2008. Human Genome Project Information: DNA Forensics. http://www.ornl.gov/sci/techre sources/Human_Genome/elsi/forensics.shtml (accessed February 10, 2008).

Vector1Media. 2008. New Uses for Soil Databases. http://vector1media.com/ article/feature/dirty-work-%96-new-uses-for-soil-databases/ (accessed February 10, 2008).

Walsh-Henry, Heather, Cheryl Katzmarzyk and Anthony B. Falsetti. 1999. Identification of Human Skeletal Remains: Was He a She or She a He. In *Forensic Osteological Analysis: A Book of Case Studies,* ed. Scott Fairgrievc, 17–35. Springfield, IL: Charles C. Thomas.

Westindiantimes.net. 2006. Caribbean Headline News Roundup. http://www .westindiantimes.net/nws/64.html (accessed February 6, 2008).

Willey, O., and Alan Heilman. 1987. Estimating Time Since Death Using Plant Roots and Stems. *Journal of Forensic Sciences* 32 (5): 1263–70.

3

Computer Forensics
Tools and Practices for the Caribbean

SHEAU-DONG **LANG** and NAZIR **ALLADIN**

Computers and, more generally, digital devices are routinely being linked to crime-scene investigations. Computers (or digital devices) may play the role of the instrument of a crime, a target, a repository of data related to crime, or combinations of the above. Computer forensics deals with the investigation and analysis of digital evidence in the context of law, and is performed by trained examiners using specialized software and hardware tools. In this chapter, we describe the major steps of computer forensic examination, techniques and tools, and current best practices used in the trade. An attempt will be made to explore the usefulness of computer forensics within the context of rising crime in the Caribbean region.

Introduction

As personal computers and access to the Internet become more prevalent, societies are increasingly becoming dependent on the computer and networking technologies for storing, processing, and sharing data, and for e-mail and message communication. The proliferation of computers has made computer-based systems and computer networks easy targets for criminal activities. According to Sergeant Kevin Stenger of Florida's Orange County Sheriff's Office, an experienced computer crime investigator in law enforcement: "Computer crimes were originally thought of just in the terms of hackers and virus makers, mainly due to the fact that at first only a few geeks had access to computers, but now anyone can point and click and use a computer to commit just about any crime" (Sheriff's Offices 2007).

Issues which will be explored in this chapter are as follows:

1. What types of crimes are being committed with computers?
2. What information is generated to corroborate the facts and circumstances of computer crime investigation?
3. What tools and procedures are used by computer forensic examiners to articulate the relevant data?

However, given the importance of computer forensics to this chapter, a brief definition of this concept is required.

What Is Computer Forensics?

Computer forensics can be defined as the application of science and engineering to the legal problem of digital evidence (Sammes and Jenkinson 2000). Computer forensics is largely a response to a demand for service from the law enforcement community (Noblett et al. 2000). The term "computer forensics" was coined in 1991 in the first training session held by the International Association of Computer Investigative Specialists in Portland, Oregon (Marcella and Greenfield 2002). Computer forensics involves the following steps regarding the handling of computer data or digital evidence (Kruse and Heiser 2002):

Preservation – the acquisition of data within legal constraints that constitute evidence without tampering.

Identification – the labelling of each item of evidence, which involves bagging and tagging, identifying with case number, descriptions, date and time of evidence collection, and signatures of handlers.

Extraction – the authentication of evidence using hash values, forensic tools and established procedures for data analysis, keyword searches, and hex and graphics viewers. It is also necessary to establish a timeline of events, locate corroborating evidence and answer the who-what-when-where-why-how questions.

Documentation – the logging of steps and actions taken during the investigation, writing a forensic report and exporting copies of notable evidences.

Interpretation – the presentation to the court as an examiner or expert witness of the evidence.

The reference (Phillips et al. 2005) is a good source on the historical accounts of computer forensics developments over the period since the early 1980s.

Computers from Crime Scenes

Computers and other digital devices (such as cell phones, digital cameras and personal digital assistants [PDAs]) are routinely involved in crime cases such as burglary, identity theft, embezzlement, fraudulent use of credit cards, domestic violence, stalking, bomb threats, hacking, prostitution, gambling, narcotics, money laundering, counterfeiting checks, homicide, suicide, child pornography, child exploitation, missing persons and so on. A prime example is an auto theft case that occurred in Florida (Sheriff's Offices 2007). Several auto thefts occurred in a five-mile radius in which Honda and Acura vehicles were stolen. The investigations revealed that stolen cars were being sent to South Florida and disassembled. One of several suspects was arrested for the incidents and his computer seized after consent was given. The problem faced by the investigator and forensics examiner was to identify and corroborate evidence that the suspect was communicating with members of an auto theft ring, and to look for evidence of stolen auto parts being sold on the Internet. Finally, after the investigation was completed, several other individuals were identified from the suspect's e-mail address book. Evidence recovered indicates that the suspects were "chopping" cars and selling the parts online at various sites. As a result, several cases from Orlando to Miami were solved.

In the Caribbean, computer forensics needs to be increasingly applied in crime solving because of the high level of criminality in the region. Bryan (2000) identified several types of transnational organized crimes in the Caribbean including drug trafficking, money laundering, terrorism, human trafficking, theft of intellectual property and computer crime, among others. According to Bryan, in order to facilitate their criminal activities, transnational organized crime groups make use of excellent communications: disposable mobile phones, phone cards and the Internet. However, Caribbean countries are especially vulnerable to this level of transnational criminal intrusion because of their geography, small size, growing culture of corruption, general tardiness of response and lack of financial resources to keep pace with rapid technological advances.

A concrete crime example was reported in the British newspaper the *Guardian* (Seager 2006), which stated that the estimate of attempted "carousel" fraud on value-added tax (VAT) was £300 million in October 2006, down significantly from £5 billion a month in 2005, after the closure of a Caribbean bank used by organized criminals for fraud. This type of fraud occurs when fraudsters import goods such as mobile phones free of VAT, then sell them to another dealer with the VAT added, but then the VAT "goes missing" and is never handed over to Britain's Revenue and Customs Office. Carousel fraud occurs when a ring of fraudsters pass the goods on between them, re-exporting them to reclaim VAT, then re-importing them again. The newspaper article reported that fraudsters used sophisticated computer programmes to create "virtual" trades without actually moving goods. In September 2006, the Dutch government closed down the First Curaçao International Bank, which was the bank used by all of the United Kingdom's carousel fraudsters.

A recent article (Caribbean Net News 2007) cited concerns about the seriousness of cyber crimes in Suriname. Suriname's justice minister told the parliament that it is extremely difficult to track down individuals who are committing Internet fraud or other forms of cyber crime. Two cyber crime cases were cited in the article: one involved a website offering assistance in (illegally) obtaining, for large sums of money, official Surinamese documents such as passports, birth certificates and so on; the other case involved the National Party of Suriname's website being hijacked and turned into a pornographic site.

Williams (2007) has highlighted the ongoing credit card fraud problem in Trinidad and Tobago coupled with the lack of cyber laws to effectively combat the problem. The article listed various types of credit card fraud, such as unauthorized use, mail theft, identity theft and fraudulent applications, and also described two existing laws fighting fraud: the Electronic Transfer of Funds Crime Act 2000 of Trinidad and Tobago, which was amended by Act No. 19 of 2005, and the Computer Misuse Act 2000. Williams pointed out that the law regarding credit cards is critically needed, and the law enforcement machinery needs to be upgraded to assist in the investigation and prosecution of credit card fraudsters.

A joint report published in 2007 on crime development in the Caribbean (United Nations and the World Bank 2007) cited increased criminal activities in narcotics trafficking, money laundering and financial fraud. In all of these cases, computers and digital devices apparently played a significant role. The report also cited recommendations for modernizing the police, with one important recommendation being the increased use of technology in crime prevention and detection.

Computer (Digital) Forensics Tools

Over the years, a number of computer forensics tools have been engineered as part of our crime-fighting toolkit. These tools include disk editors (viewers), which can recover "deleted" files, and disk imaging facilities to duplicate disks. Some tools can also recognize fragments of special files based on file signatures (header information). As computer systems become more complex and new applications are developed, sophisticated computer forensics tools with a graphical user interface (GUI) have now entered the mainstream marketplace in order to effectively handle larger amounts of disk storage and data. These tools have enabled forensic examiners to achieve the following:

- Recover previously deleted files and folders
- Recognize disk partitions and common file systems (Windows FAT and NTFS, Linux ext2 and ext3, Unix UFS)
- Carve graphics and other files of known signatures from unallocated disk clusters
- Search strings using regular expressions
- Review registry files (on Microsoft Windows systems)
- Recover user passwords
- Recover e-mail and instant messages (IMs)
- Provide timelines of file access activities based on date/time stamps
- Identify known files based on hash sets
- Identify artefacts specific to the operating system on disk

We will be describing these features in greater detail in this chapter, mainly using AccessData's Forensic Toolkit FTK (AccessData) as an example. We will also comment on two other tools: Guidance Software's EnCase (Guidance Software) and Brian Carrier's The Sleuthkit TSK (Carrier). Other computer forensics software tools not discussed here, due to lack of space, include ProDiscover (http://www.techpathways.com/), X-Ways (http://www.winhex.com/), and many open-source tools that are Windows or Linux-based (http://www.opensourceforensics.org/). In this chapter our discussions will be heavily focused on Microsoft Windows systems, which are the most frequently encountered operating system, given Microsoft's market dominance.

Forensic Workstation and Hardware

Professional forensic examiners use high-end computers (or laptops) as their forensic workstations. One example is the commercial forensic workstation Forensic Recovery of Evidence Device (FRED), from Digital Intelligence (http://www.digitalintelligence.com), which has the following highlights:

- Intel Core 2 Duo processor with 4GigaBytes of RAM
- Disk trays for ATA, SATA, SCSI drives with write-blocker to acquire disk images
- Reader for compact flash, micro drives, smart media, memory stick and other multimedia cards
- Triple-boot operating system (DOS 6.22, Win98 DOS and Windows XP Pro)

A write-blocker is the electronics that connects to a suspect's drive on one end and to the forensic workstation on the other end. The purpose of the write-blocker is to allow read-only access to the suspect's drive. This ensures no alternation to the drive's contents while the disk image is being acquired. A write-blocker is a necessary piece of hardware. Some of the write-blockers on the market include: FastBloc from Guidance Software and FireFly from Digital Intelligence, among others. A website sponsored by the Computer Forensics Tools Testing project of the US National Institute of Science and Technology (http://www .cftt.nist.gov/hardware_write_block.htm) contains useful testing results of write-blockers.

Data Acquisition

Digital evidence may exist in a variety of forms and media. One of the first steps in forensic examination is to extract digital evidence relevant to the case under investigation. The procedures and tools used in data acquisition must be scientifically (forensically) sound and well documented, using best practice standards, so the examination results may be presented in the court of law for cross examination and challenges by the opposing counsel.

Acquiring Live System Data

Digital evidence may be extracted from a "live" system while the system is still running or from a "dead" system when the power has been turned off. Live system acquisition is appropriate, and sometimes even necessary, such as in a business environment where the computer servers cannot easily be shutdown without adversely affecting the business operation. In such cases, the forensic investigator will probably need to work with system administrators to gain administrative access to the server and extract relevant data by copying files and folders from individual user's accounts and from system folders. On-site data filtering may be used to limit the scope of data extraction to only the relevant data and to reduce the amount of copied data. The collected data are then taken back to the laboratory for detailed examination and analysis. Live analysis tools may also be used to take snapshots of the computer's random access memory (RAM), which contains information about currently running applications (at least the portions that are currently loaded in the RAM). Images of the RAM may also contain user passwords and decrypted data.

A free tool for live system analysis of Microsoft Windows systems is the Helix CD distributed by e-defense.com (http://www.e-fense .com/helix). The Helix CD packages a collection of third-party software tools for incident response and electronic discovery. One way to use the Helix CD is to run it on a live Windows system. When Helix is first run, an initial screen warns the user of changes to be made to the underlying system. After accepting this condition, a GUI displays the choices of tools and documents available (see figure 3.1 for a screenshot). It is understood that since the system is live (running), the acquired information represents a snapshot accurate only at certain point of time.

The available options for live acquisition using Helix are as follows:

- System information that can identify operating system, owner, network IP address and attached drives.
- System acquisition that can acquire images of RAM and attached physical drives or logical file systems using Windows-based data dump tool dd or the FTK Imager software (from AccessData).

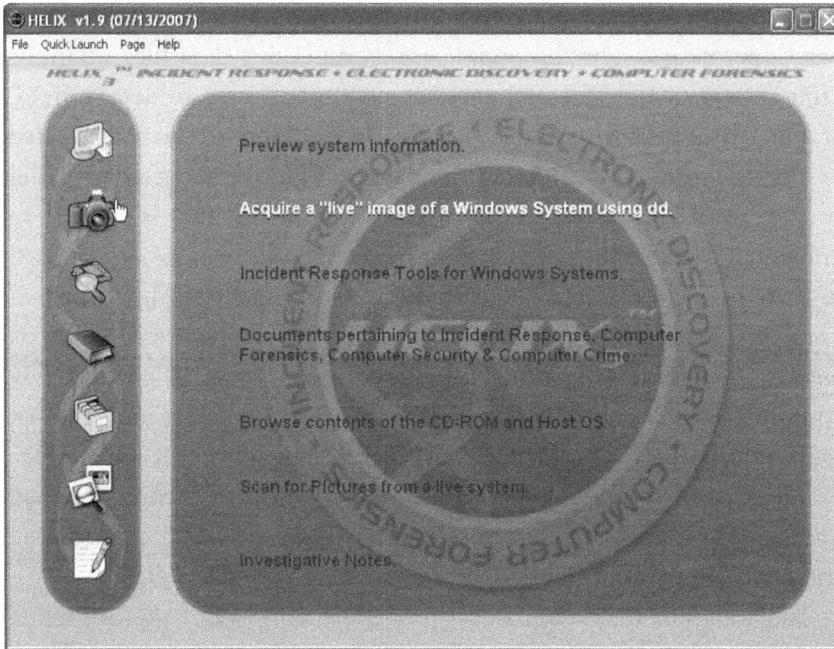

Figure 3.1
Helix (v. 1.9) inter-
face in a live system
(with "Acquisition"
highlighted). (All
images in chapter
supplied by Sheau-
Dong Lang.)

- Incident response tools that contain a list of third-party tools for extracting passwords, viewing browser history and cookies, system auditing, detecting rootkits, viewing registry files, viewing connected USB devices and so on.
- Browsing files and folders that allow a scan for pictures and can compose investigative notes.

When exiting the Helix environment, an optional log file is generated that details individual steps performed during investigation including the time stamps, and the contents of the investigative notes. The log file can be a very useful part of the forensic report.

Acquiring Hard Disk Data

It is more common for investigators and forensic examiners to acquire data from powered-down hard disks or other media (CDs, DVDs, thumb drives, tapes and so on) and digital devices (cell phones, PDAs, digital cameras and so on) involved in a case under investigation. We will first describe the tools and procedures used in acquiring data of a hard disk.

Hard disks are the most commonly used devices for storing the computer operating system, user applications, and other data files, all in the same media. Data files include user documents and folders, e-mail, graphics files (pictures, audio and video files), and artefacts generated by the operating system and applications. The operating system files contain information such as user ID and password that is specific to individual users of the computer (or laptop), and therefore can be used to link the hard disk data and evidence of activities to the identified users during investigation. Typically, when a file or folder is deleted, its data content still exists on the disk. Also, unallocated disk clusters may contain remnants of deleted documents, graphics files, messages or snapshots of the RAM. Hence, hard disk acquisition tools make a bit-by-bit copy of the disk and verify the image integrity using matched hash values. It is extremely critical that the hard disk data are acquired and analysed without tampering of evidence on the disk.

The standard disk acquisition procedure consists of the following steps:

1. Preparing a "storage" disk. This involves selecting a hard disk of equal, or preferably larger, size than the "target" drive of which you want to make an image; the storage disk is sterilized by zeroing out all bytes.

2. Connecting drives. This entails connecting the target drive to a write-blocker, and then connecting the write-blocker to the forensic computer. This guarantees no alternation to the target drive during data acquisition process. The storage drive should subsequently be connected to your forensic computer.

3. Disk imaging. This involves starting your forensic computer into Windows, making sure that both the storage and target drives are mounted. A forensic disk-imaging tool such as Accessdata's Disk Imager is then executed in order to create a disk image of the target drive.

4. Checking image integrity. After the imaging is complete, the imaging tool is used to verify that the target drive and the image have the same hash values (MD5 and SHA1), guaranteeing that a bit-by-bit image has in fact been created. The target drive from the forensic computer is subsequently disconnected and returned to the evidence locker. At all times the forensic examination is performed on the created image file.

There are alternative disk imaging tools. For example, the Helix CD contains a Linux-based disk-imaging tool called LinEn, from Guidance Software. There are times when the target drive may be difficult to remove from the original (suspect's) computer or when the forensic computer does not recognize the target drive. In that case, it is possible to run Helix on the suspect's computer by connecting the storage disk to it. You must ensure, when attempting to boot the suspect's computer into Helix, that great care is taken to avoid booting the computer from the suspect's hard drive (which would immediately modify many system files and affect their date and time stamps). This is accomplished by first disconnecting the power from the suspect's hard drive and turning the computer on to verify that the boot sequence in its BIOS settings is booting from CD before booting from hard disk (and to disable booting from hard disk completely if BIOS supports it). Once the boot sequence is set properly, reconnect power to the suspect's hard disk and then turn the computer on to boot into Helix.

There is yet another scenario to use Helix: booting the suspect's computer into Helix but without connecting the storage disk to the suspect's computer. Instead, use a network crossover cable to connect the suspect's computer and the forensic computer, and attach the storage disk to the forensic computer. The suspect's computer should then be booted into Helix. Run LinEn to acquire the target disk via the network crossover cable. The reference book (Bunting and Wei 2006) contains detailed instructions on how to use LinEn in network acquisition.

Acquiring Data from Other Digital Media

Digital evidence and data often exist in media other than computer hard disk. Many (or most) criminals have cell phones that contain contact information, recently called numbers, text messages, pictures and, possibly, videos. Digital cameras are also commonly used devices for committing crime. Usually, special software tools and cables are needed to connect to, and acquire data directly from, these digital devices. The article (Ayers et al. 2005) reports studies of forensic software tools for a number of popular cellular phone platforms, including Symbian, RIM (Research In Motion), Pocket PC and Palm OS devices. The article describes various scenarios in which the tools are used and summarizes the findings. A companion article (Jansen and Ayers 2007) discusses procedures for the preservation, acquisition, examination, analysis and reporting of digital information present on cell phones, as well as available forensic software tools that support those activities.

Data Analysis

After the target disk has been acquired, the disk image should be examined in order to detect digital evidence relevant to the case under investigation. Forensic examiners typically are given some background information from the investigator (case agent) that will assist the forensic examiner. These are things like names, addresses, time window, types of files (spreadsheets, pictures, movies) and installed applications. Experienced examiners know which files, folders and Windows registries to scrutinize for relevant evidence, how to corroborate evidences, and how to get the most out of forensic tools.

AccessData's FTK

The Forensic Toolkit (FTK) from AccessData is one of the more popular computer forensics tools used by the examiners. FTK provides a very intuitive interface when an acquired disk image is loaded into a new case. This can be seen in figure 3.2. The top menu bar provides six option tabs: Overview, Explore, Graphics, E-mail, Search and Book-

Figure 3.2
The initial screen ("Overview" tab selected) for an open case in FTK

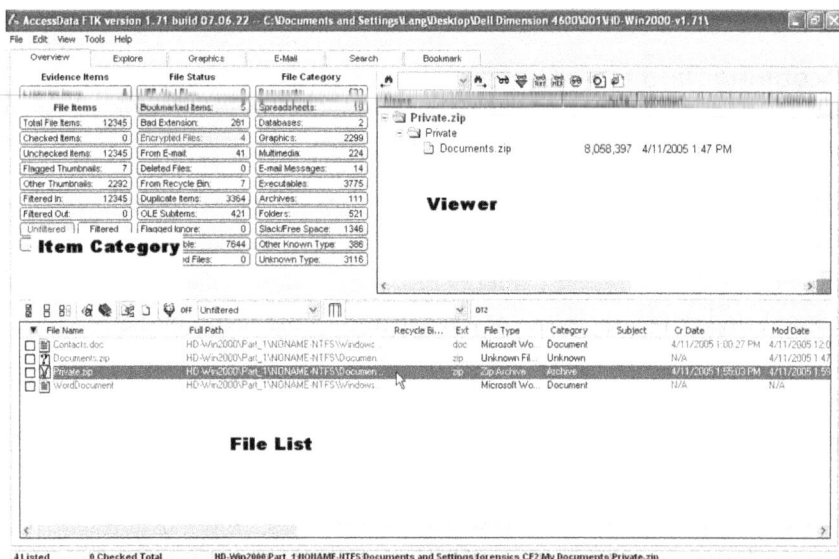

SHEAU-DONG **LANG** and NAZIR **ALLADIN**

mark. In figure 3.2, the "Overview" tab is selected by default, giving an overview in terms of total number of items in different categories (e-mail, deleted files, documents, spreadsheets, encrypted files and so on). When an item category is selected, files within that category are shown in the lower area, which enables the selected file to be viewed in the upper-right viewer area.

The "Explore" tab may be used to browse through the directory tree. The contents of any selected file can be viewed in the file viewer area.

Figure 3.3 shows an example of the directory of graphics files when the "Graphics" tab is selected. Additional pane areas present the thumbnail view, file listing and detailed view of a selected graphics file (as highlighted).

When the "E-mail" tab is selected, a directory tree of e-mail folders is displayed. Other pane areas display the list of messages for the selected e-mail folder, the actual message in human-readable form for selected message and the e-mail's attachments. During forensic examination, items of interest may be selected and bookmarked. Bookmarked items may be grouped into different bookmark names. Properties of book-marked items may be saved, with the Bookmark tab from the top menu bar subsequently used to view currently bookmarked items. These items can easily be incorporated into the forensic report.

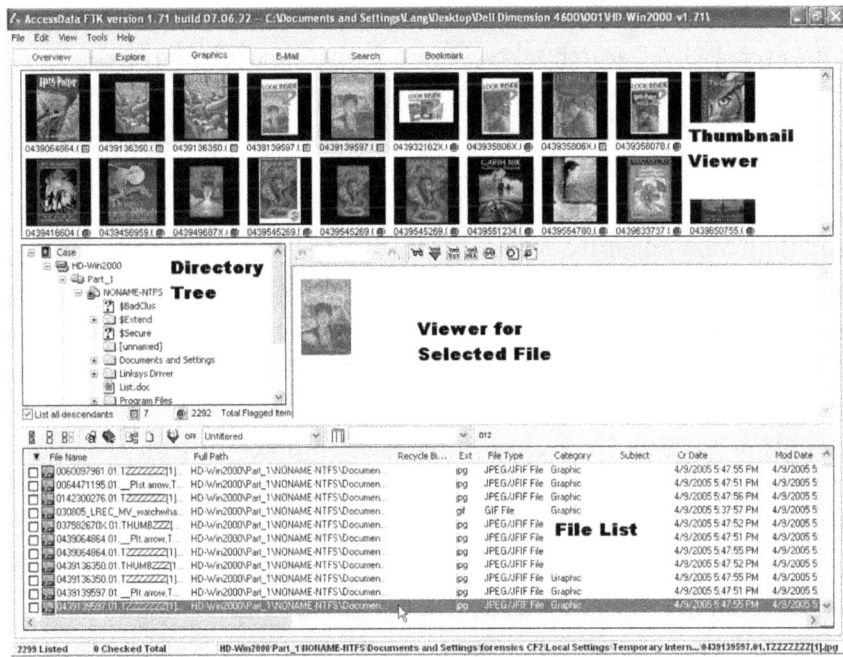

Figure 3.3
Graphics tab selected for an open case in FTK

Figure 3.4
Search results in
FTK

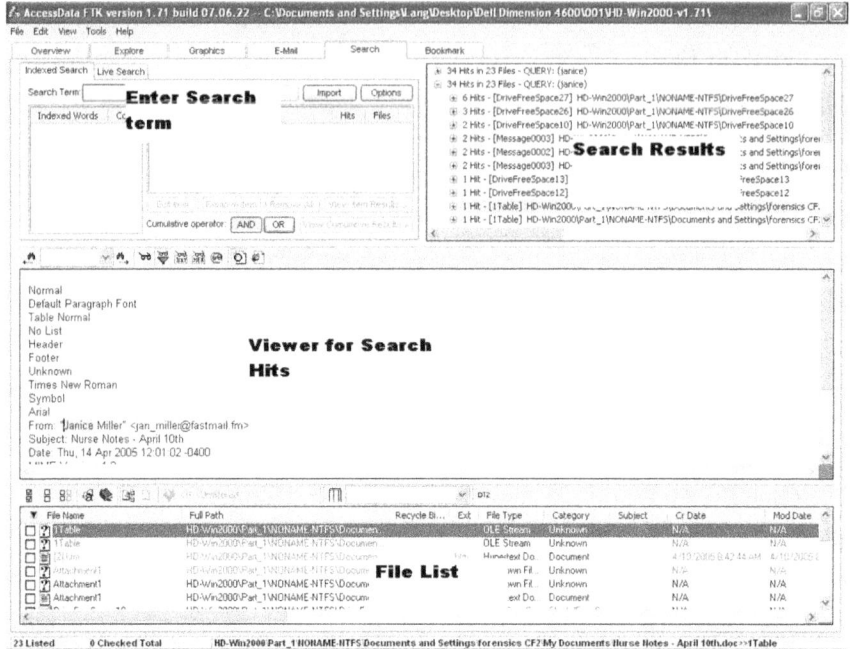

Figure 3.4 shows the interface for conducting string (or regular expression) searches and the search results under the "Search" tab. Search terms may be entered to perform an indexed search which returns results quickly based on pre-computed indexes. "Live" searches can also be conducted for both words and regular expressions. However, a "live" search takes a much longer time to complete.

Other Forensics Tools

Another comprehensive forensics tool is Guidance Software's EnCase (Guidance Software). Figure 3.5 shows a screenshot of the EnCase's interface. An Internet Explorer's history folder is selected from the "Tree" pane, and a particular JPEG file of that history is highlighted in the "Table" pane. The "Table" pane is used to sort files and show various file properties. The picture of the selected JPEG file is shown in the "View" pane on the lower left. The "Filter" pane on the lower right can be used to select filtering conditions by running pre-packaged EnScripts from Guidance Software, an extremely powerful and flexible feature of EnCase. Similar to FTK, EnCase can be used to extract graphics files, e-mail, perform string searches and generate reports.

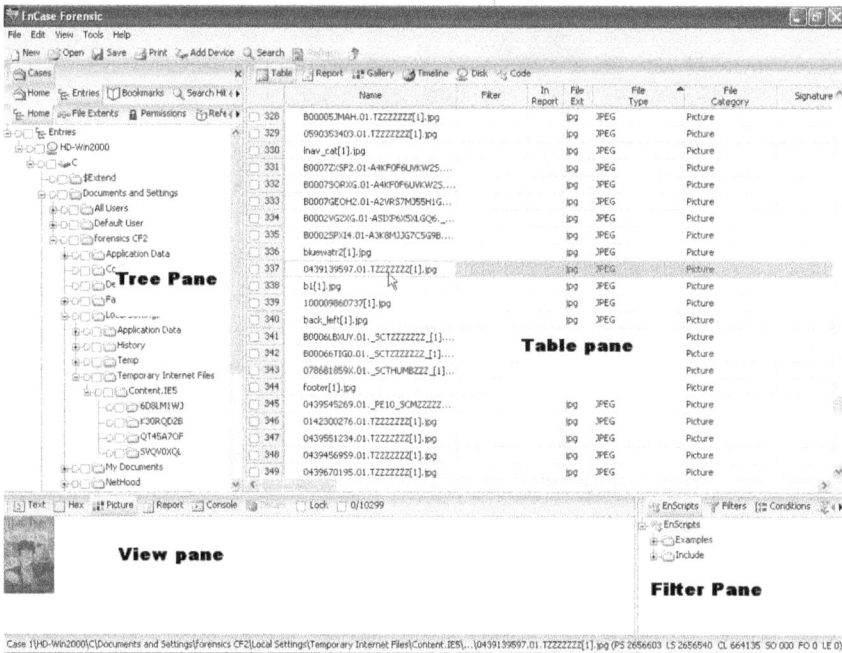

Figure 3.5
Guidance
Software's EnCase

An open-source forensic tool that runs on Unix platforms is The Sleuthkit (TSK) and its GUI frontend Autopsy (Carrier). TSK/Autopsy understands Windows and UNIX disks and file systems (NTFS, FAT, UFS1/2, Ext2/3), and it provides facilities for listing files and directories (including those that have been deleted)and viewing file contents. It also can perform file access timeline analysis, file metadata analysis, disk and file layouts, and keyword searches. TSK/Autopsy also provides audit logs that record exact TSK commands used and steps taken by the examiner, and it allows notes entered during examination to be used in the final report. A sample screenshot of TSK/Autopsy showing the layout for file analysis is given in figure 3.6.

Forensic Report

Forensic tools typically provide a report generation wizard that helps create reports based on the examination work. Figure 3.7 shows an example report produced by FTK, which is an HTML file with hyperlinks connected to items identified during the examination including case information, bookmarks, flagged graphics, search results, directory and file listing, file properties to be included, copies of files to be

Figure 3.6
TSK/Autopsy's interface for file analysis

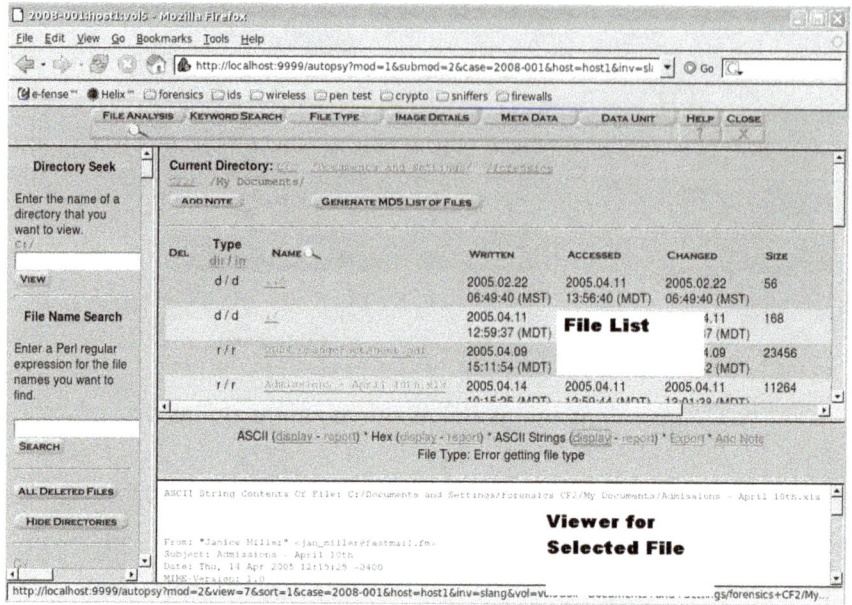

Figure 3.7
An example of an FTK report

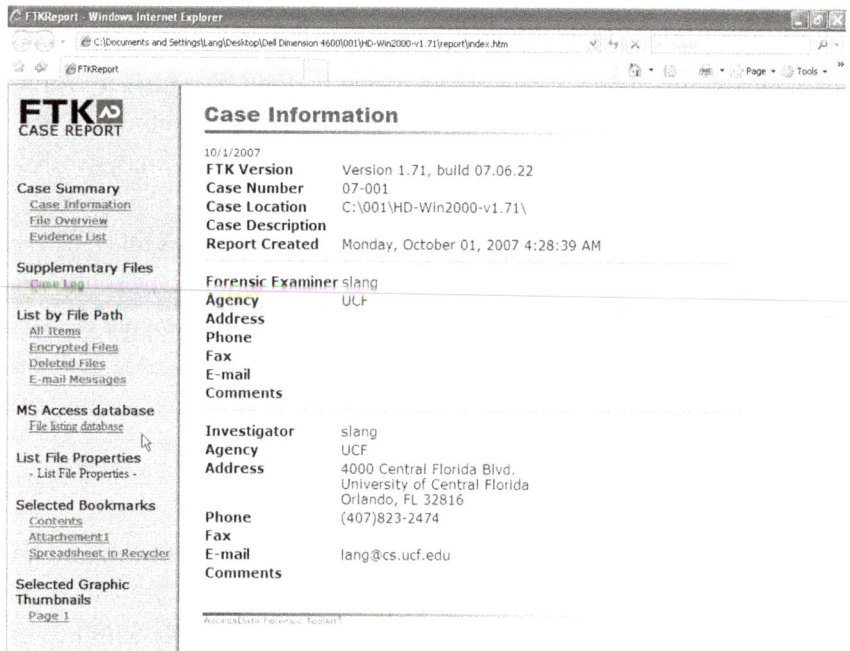

exported and be available with the report, and a detailed case log showing steps and operations taken during examination. The report, along with associated files, can be copied to CD or DVD and submitted to the case agent.

Most agencies have their own format requirements and presentation guidelines for forensic reports. The forensic examiners would export the examination results created by a forensic tool such as FTK, make required adjustments and compile the final forensic report. A sample template for forensic reports contains the following sections (Sheriff's Offices 2007):

Identification: Identify the agency name, case number, case agent, date, and forensic examiner's information

About the Report: An administrative section to explain software tools such as video file viewer, and links to downloading sites, to view contents of the report

Pre-examination and Acquisition: Briefly explain the case and scope of examination; for pre-examination describe the handling of the devices, chain of custody, documenting make/model/serial numbers, CMOS settings such as boot sequence, system date/time; for acquisition discuss forensic tools used, integrity of image files verified by hash values using hyperlinks to reports produced by forensic software (FTK or EnCase)

Examination of Evidence and Report: Discuss results of examination; you may use the reports generated by forensic software and hyperlink to them; examples of findings include: time zone settings (with link to registry information extracted by forensic software); notable files bookmarked using software and links to the details; notable entries in Internet history files with links to more details.

Summary: Summarize the examination results by discussing the nexus between discovered artefacts and how they help to articulate the issues under investigation.

Hypothetical Case

In order to demonstrate how computer forensics tools can be usefully applied, we will discuss the sequence of events relating to the following hypothetical criminal case.

Case Study

The US Immigration and Customs Enforcement (ICE) Office receives a tip that a Florida man owns child pornographic materials on his home computer and the materials were purchased by mail from a Trinidad address. The ICE agents apply to the judge and receive a search warrant given the probable cause. Working together, the ICE agents and local sheriff deputies serve the search warrant at the suspect's residence and take a laptop computer, some CDs and DVDs, and some mailing packages sent from a Trinidad address. The materials are properly tagged and bagged, and subsequently taken back to the sheriff's office Computer Crime Lab for forensic examination. Back in the sheriff's office computer crime laboratory, the hard disk from the suspect's laptop computer is removed. Identification information of the laptop's model, the hard disk's model, size and serial number are recorded on the case inventory form. A sterilized storage disk (a disk containing only binary value zeros), larger than the capacity of suspect's disk, is prepared and then configured with the Windows FAT32 file system. The forensic examiner connects the storage disk to the forensic workstation and connects the suspect's hard disk to a write-blocker, which is then connected to the forensic workstation. The AccessData's FTK Imager is used to make a bit-by-bit image of the suspect's disk. Hash values are then computed to verify the integrity of the image (that is, to ensure the image is an identical copy of the original). The CDs and DVDs from the suspect's residence are also imaged and copied to the forensic workstation. After completing the imaging process, the suspect's disk, CDs and DVDs are taken to the lab's evidence locker.

A forensic report is compiled based on the examination done using the forensics tool FTK. The report contains the laptop's internal clock value and time zone information, and relevant files (pictures, videos, e-mail, Internet activities) with their date and time stamps showing the creation, modification, and access times. Notable files are also copied to the CDs and given to the ICE case agent. In addition, the postal mailing address in Trinidad and the IP addresses of the websites registered to Trinidad's ISP are included. All this is then sent to the Trinidad law enforcement to pursue legal action. The suspect in the United States pleads guilty and is sentenced to jail time on charges of possession and transmission of child pornography, after the evidence is presented to his attorney. Similarly, computer forensics work is performed on the computers belonging to the suspect in Trinidad who is connected to the shipped child pornographic materials. Evidences are found that corroborated with those obtained from the ICE agents. The Trinidadian is prosecuted under the laws of Trinidad and Tobago, Sexual Offences Act No. 31 of 2000 where the legislation does not specifically pertain to child pornography, but to all pornographic material.

Conclusion

In this chapter, we have described computer forensics in the context of crime investigation and outlined the major tasks involved in computer forensic examination, illustrated by the use of forensics tools. The Caribbean, as a gateway to the Americas, is currently used as a major trans-shipment point by the drug barons of the South American mainland. Caribbean governments are all working closely with major crime-fighting organizations throughout the world to stamp out the drug trade and its related criminal activities. The use of the Internet for communication and e-commerce activities are more prevalent in completing business transactions. It is therefore quite evident that the field of computer forensics will become more important in the battle against crime. The reliance on the use of technologies as well as the understanding of the legal procedures in order to fight increasingly more sophisticated cyber criminals is available. Computer forensic examiners are critically needed to serve businesses and law enforcement agencies. Only proper education, training, and collaboration and cooperation between government agencies and business communities will ensure success in fighting computer crimes.

References

AccessDatal. The Forensic Toolkit (FTK). http://www.accessdata.com.

Ayers, R., W. Jansen, N. Cilleros and R. Daniellou, 2005. Cell Phone Forensic Tools: An Overview and Analysis. http://csrc.nist.gov/publications/nistir/nistir-7250.pdf.

Bryan, Anthony T. 2000. Transnational Organized Crime: The Caribbean Context. The Dante B. Fascell North-South Center Working Paper Series, Working Paper no. 1. October. http://www.ciaonet.org/wps/bry01/WP1ATB.pdf.

Bunting, Steve, and William Wei. 2006. *EnCase Computer Forensics: The Official EnCE: EnCase Certified Examiner Study Guide.* Indianapolis: Wiley.

Cairo, Ivan. 2007. Fighting Cyber Crime Is Huge Challenge for Suriname. *Caribbean Net News.* January 16. http://www.caribbeannetnews.com/cgi-script/csArticles/articles/000051/005145.htm.

Carrier, B. The Sleuthkit (TSK) and Autopsy. http://www.sleuthkit.org/.

Guidance Software. EnCase. http://www.guidancesoftware.com.

Jansen, W., and R. Ayers. 2007. Guidelines on Cell Phone Forensics. National Institute of Standards and Technology, United States Department of Commerce. http://csrc.nist.gov/publications/nistpubs/800-101/SP800-101.pdf.

Kruse, Warren G. II, and Jay G. Heiser. 2002. *Computer Forensics.* Boston: Addison-Wesley.

Marcella, Albert J., Jr., and Robert S. Greenfield. 2002. *Cyber Forensics: A Field Manual for Collecting, Examining, and Preserving Evidence of Computer Crimes.* 2nd ed. New York: Auerbach.

Noblett, Michael G., Mark M. Pollitt and Lawrence A. Presley. 2000. Recovering and Examining Computer Forensic Evidence. *Forensic Science Communications* 2 (4): 1–13.

Phillips, A., B. Nelson, F. Enfinger and C. Steuart. 2005. *Guide to Computer Forensics and Investigations.* 2nd ed. Boston: Course Technology.

Sammes, T., and B. Jenkinson. 2000. *Forensic Computing.* Berlin: Springer-Verlag.

Seager, Ashley. 2006. VAT Fraud Falls by £200m after Caribbean Bank Is Closed. *Guardian.* December 12. http://www.guardian.co.uk/business/2006/dec/12/money.scamsandfraud.

Sheriff's Offices of Orange and Seminole Counties. 2007. Overview of Computer Crime. Presentation.

United Nations Office on Drugs and Crime (UNODC) and the World Bank. 2007. Crime, Violence, and Development: Trends, Costs, and Policy Options in the Caribbean. http://siteresources.worldbank.org/INTHAITI/Resources/Crimeandvio lenceinthecaribbeanfullreport.pdf.

Williams, Dave Arthur. 2007. Credit Card Fraud in Trinidad and Tobago. *Journal of Financial Crime* 14 (3): 340–59.

4

Spatial Tools for Fighting Crime
The Use of Geospatial Technologies in Crime-Fighting in Jamaica

PARRIS **LYEW-AYEE**

Given the complexities involved in fighting crime, ranging from police or military action, forensic analyses, social intervention and planning, academic research, and so on, more specialized tools are evolving and being deployed to assist with the growing problem of crime in Jamaica. This chapter focuses on the spatial dimension of crime and the tools used to analyse crime patterns and trends, utilizing these technologies to actively fighting crime. The spatial dimension of crime has many different scales, and the approach to crime fighting heavily depends on knowing which scale is most appropriate. Macro-level crime fighting may look at country- or parish-wide scales. The police may have operational regions or divisions that encompass multiple police stations and administrative boundaries. These require a different level of focus than looking at more detailed station- or community-level scales. Time scales are also important; trends and patterns vary depending on time of day, day of week, month or year. The analysis of the distribution of different types of crime and the deployment of frontline tools in fighting crime, as well as the cost and effectiveness of these tools, are all scale dependent. Jamaica presents many unique challenges and opportunities in the development and use of such technologies. It has the highest crime rate in the anglophone Caribbean, coupled with a politically charged environment. This chapter will evaluate the analytical and operational uses of geospatial technologies in the fight against crime in the country, looking at the advantages and challenges of their implementation. This combined study of both the analytical and operational dimensions of geospatial technologies in crime fighting also has important implications for macro-economic planning, the development of social upliftment programmes and other non-crime-fighting purposes.

Introduction

Various strategies have been developed to combat crime in Jamaica, given the complexity of the problem in the Caribbean nation. The socio-economic, cultural and political climate in Jamaica all contribute to the problem, and all of these factors need to be evaluated as we seek to combat rising crime in Jamaica. Jamaica has the highest murder rate in the world, with 59 murders per 100,000 people in 2007 (Anthony Harriott, personal communication, 2008), ahead of Guatemala (47 murders per 100,000 people), Venezuela (45 murders per 100,000 people, and Colombia (36 murders per 100,000 people). This high crime rate has both serious and direct implications for the island's present and future economic stability.

Crime is inherently spatial and, as such, its distribution across space can be readily visualized. The use of geographic information systems (GIS) allows these crimes to be mapped and presented rapidly and easily, making possible the categorization of the data for pattern detection, as well as the overlay of related non-crime data (road data, or community maps with socio-economic and demographic attributes, for example). These techniques provide graphic representations of the crime problem within a wider spatial context, in which a fairly large area of interest can be included in any analysis or operational response. Crime-fighting spatial tools may be applied in two broad ways: for analytical purposes or for operational use. Analytical tools are used to obtain a detailed understanding of a crime pattern or trend, often adding additional data for comparative purposes from which detailed statistics and other quantitative information can be derived. These data are often used for academic purposes, as well as detailed policy analyses aimed at resolving crime problems from a macro-socioeconomic perspective, involving social upliftment programmes, political intervention, and community planning and restructuring. This approach should yield more successes in the long run than merely equipping the police force with more personnel, vehicles and weapons.

Operational use of crime-fighting spatial tools involves the use of global positioning systems (GPS) for intelligence gathering, as well as coupling these data with critical information relating to pre-, during-, and post-operations briefings and coordination. Managing resource deployment and response is also facilitated through the use of GPS tracking and monitoring. These tend to be the solutions most actively sought and used by the Jamaican police, with varying levels of applications and success to date. This chapter focuses on the spatial tools used in identifying areas with high crime rates. Details on the crimes themselves are not given in this chapter due to strict confidentiality clauses. The body of research presented in this chapter will also evaluate some current operational tactics, and how these may be improved by the application of spatial tools to assist with Jamaica's crime-fighting objectives.

Analytical Tools

The analytical tools available may be used to map and model spatial and temporal patterns and trends of crime at different scales. These can then be used to compare with existing data on socio-economic conditions, demography and so on in order to explain the observed patterns and trends. These will be placed within their proper contexts for further analyses. Descriptive and derivative statistics can all be applied to crime data that have been mapped and modelled, that is, have a spatial dimension. It is often meaningless to simply report that crime rates are up or down over a particular period without a spatial context. Overall, crime statistics may improve or worsen, but local variations are not captured by this kind of generalized reporting. Parishes or communities with the highest total crimes or greatest increase in crime over a previous time period can be mapped, illustrating areas that require particular attention. The inclusion of additional data sets, such as demography, can improve the quality of the analyses. For example, demographic data can enable us to calculate the number of crimes per thousand persons or determine whether there are any correlations between crime and certain social infrastructures such as vacant lots and bars.

However, the types of analyses applied are dependent on the scale of the data, which may be spatial – at the scale of parish, police division, community or incident – or temporal – hourly, per shift, daily, weekly, monthly or annually. These are all influenced by the availability, quality and currency of the data provided. Usually, lower-resolution data (parish- or police-division–scale information released annually) are more readily available and provide some basis for initial analysis.

Police-Division Scale

In the case of Jamaica, police-division scale was the coarsest resolution used for this study. The data provided by the Jamaica Constabulary Force allowed comparisons between and among the nineteen different police divisions in the island and an assessment of the overall distribution of crimes across Jamaica. Jamaica has fourteen parishes and nineteen police divisions. In all of the parishes, except Kingston, St Andrew and St Catherine, each police division is equivalent to the parish boundary. Kingston, St Andrew and St Catherine, being the most heavily populated parishes, containing more than half the total population of Jamaica, are divided into eight police divisions.

Crime information for these divisions included type of crime, as well as time of crime and victim profiles. This information can be mapped according to the respective divisions with the data subsequently subjected to comparative analyses. Figure 4.1 shows total crimes by police division in 2006, with the victim profiles superimposed. Clearly, crime is not uniformly distributed across Jamaica, being concentrated in some police divisions more than others.

An obvious drawback to the use of police-division–scale information is that this does not isolate problem areas within the divisions. More detailed information is increasingly difficult to acquire and compile. In many cases, data from individual police stations may not be as updated or comprehensive as data from other stations. However, if this is eventually sorted out, much more meaningful information can be derived.

Community Scale

All murders in Kingston from 2000 to 2005 have been mapped (Lyew-Ayee 2006). The precise locations of these murders are not shown in this report, but the information may be related to communities (Figure 4.2) not only to identify those that have particularly high murder rates, but also to compare crime information specific to certain communities with demographic and socio-economic data (Statistical Institute of Jamaica 2003a, 2003b). These are shown in figures 4.3 and 4.4.

Kingston is divided into 108 "special areas". These are subdivisions of the city defined by an agglomeration of enumeration districts and traditional communities of which the majority are lower-middle to low

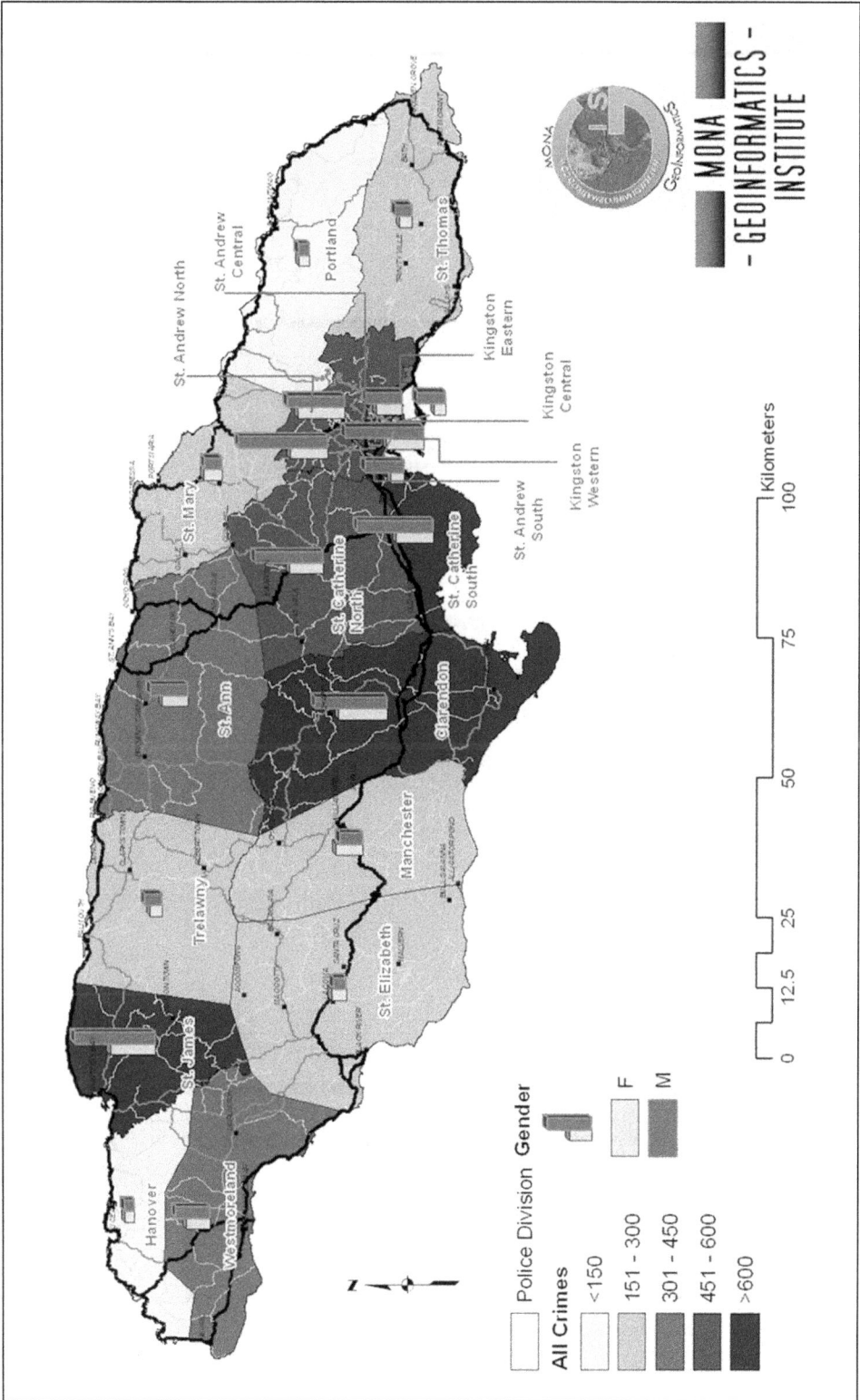

Figure 4.1 Total crimes in Jamaica in 2006 showing gender breakdown by police division

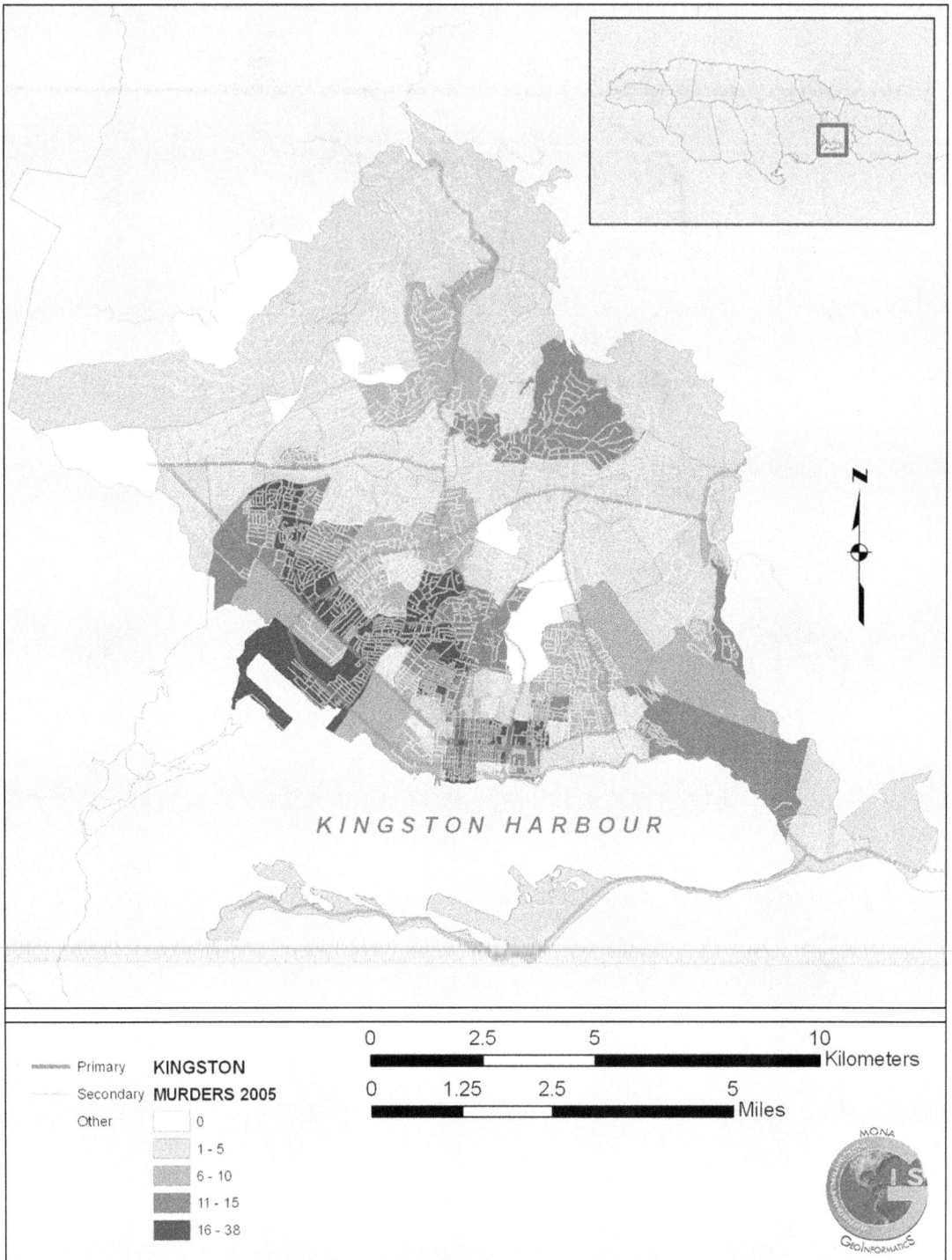

Figure 4.2 *Community map of murders in Kingston (2005)*

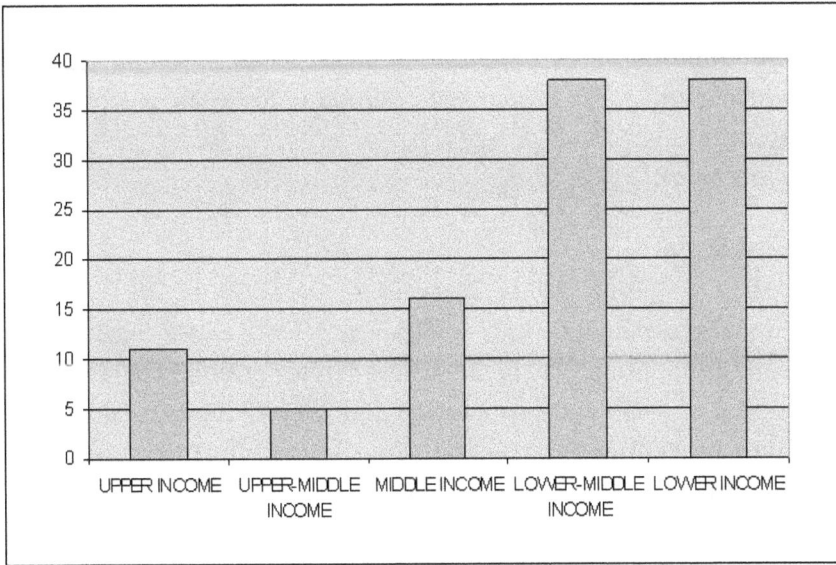

Figure 4.3
Number of com-
munities in dif-
ferent income
brackets in
Kingston

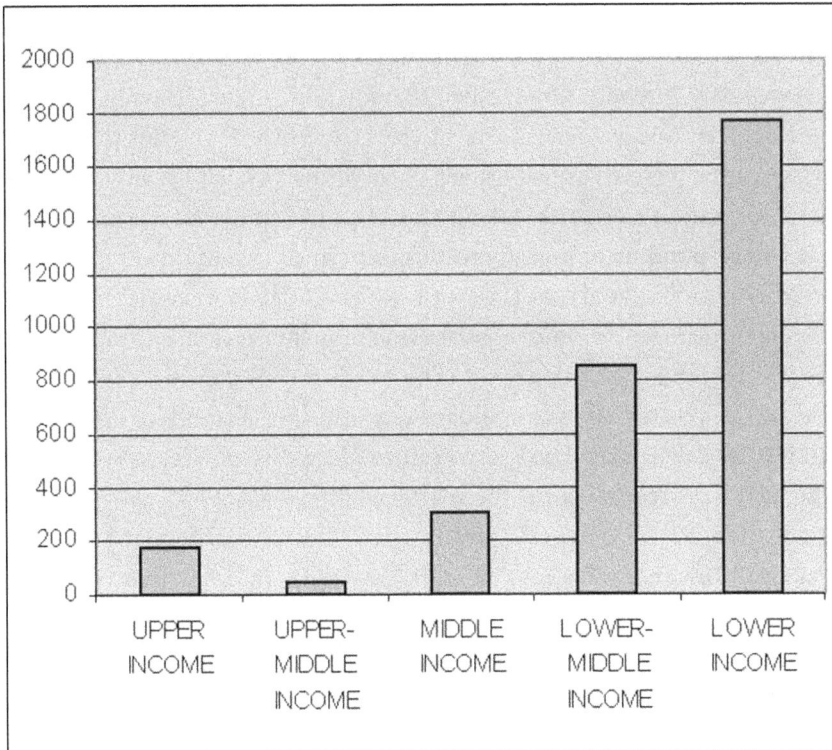

Figure 4.4
Total number of
murders
(2000–2005) in
Kingston based
on income
brackets

income. The bulk of the murders in the city occurred within these regions. While murders are not alien to higher-income communities, the overwhelming majority of murders occurred in lower-income places in Kingston.

Incident Scale

Traditionally, community-scale studies may refer to entire communities as being crime-prone. Incident-scale analyses remove the artificial boundaries of community delineation and identify the natural pattern of crimes irrespective of community boundaries. While we may not be able to directly correlate these spatial data with socio-economic or other variables, these "hot spot" models, as represented by the incident-scale analyses (for example, figure 4.5), provide a more realistic depiction of crime-ridden regions within the city. A *hot spot* can be defined as an area with more than twenty murders per square mile.

In terms of the homicide patterns, it is clear that certain parts of the Kingston metropolis are worse than others. The spatial data presented also depict areas that may be considered "warm spots" and "cool spots"; which also demonstrates that not all of Kingston is crime-ridden. Isolated "warm spots" from figure 4.5 show portions of the enclaves of Whitehall, Grant's Pen, Papine and August Town clearly in the northern and eastern parts of the city, away from the true "hot spots" of the western and southern parts of the city. The police may use this information to strategically and tactically deploy their resources in order to respond meaningfully to this pattern of criminality.

Centrographic analyses (Lee and Wong 2001; Harries 1999) show the spatial centres of point distributions, in this case all homicides in Kingston over a six-year period. The mean for all coordinates in each year can be plotted and the standard deviation – the standard distance – can also be calculated. The spatial centre of the city of Kingston is in the Half Way Tree region, while the spatial centre of murders is in the Cross Roads area, to the south. Generally, the centre of murders in Kingston is skewed towards the south of Half Way Tree. In other words, homicides in Kingston are most heavily concentrated in the southern parts of the city. The analyses of these spatial centres can also reveal whether a particular distribution is migrating over time. Over the six-year period of analysis, murders were not migrating in any other direction as the

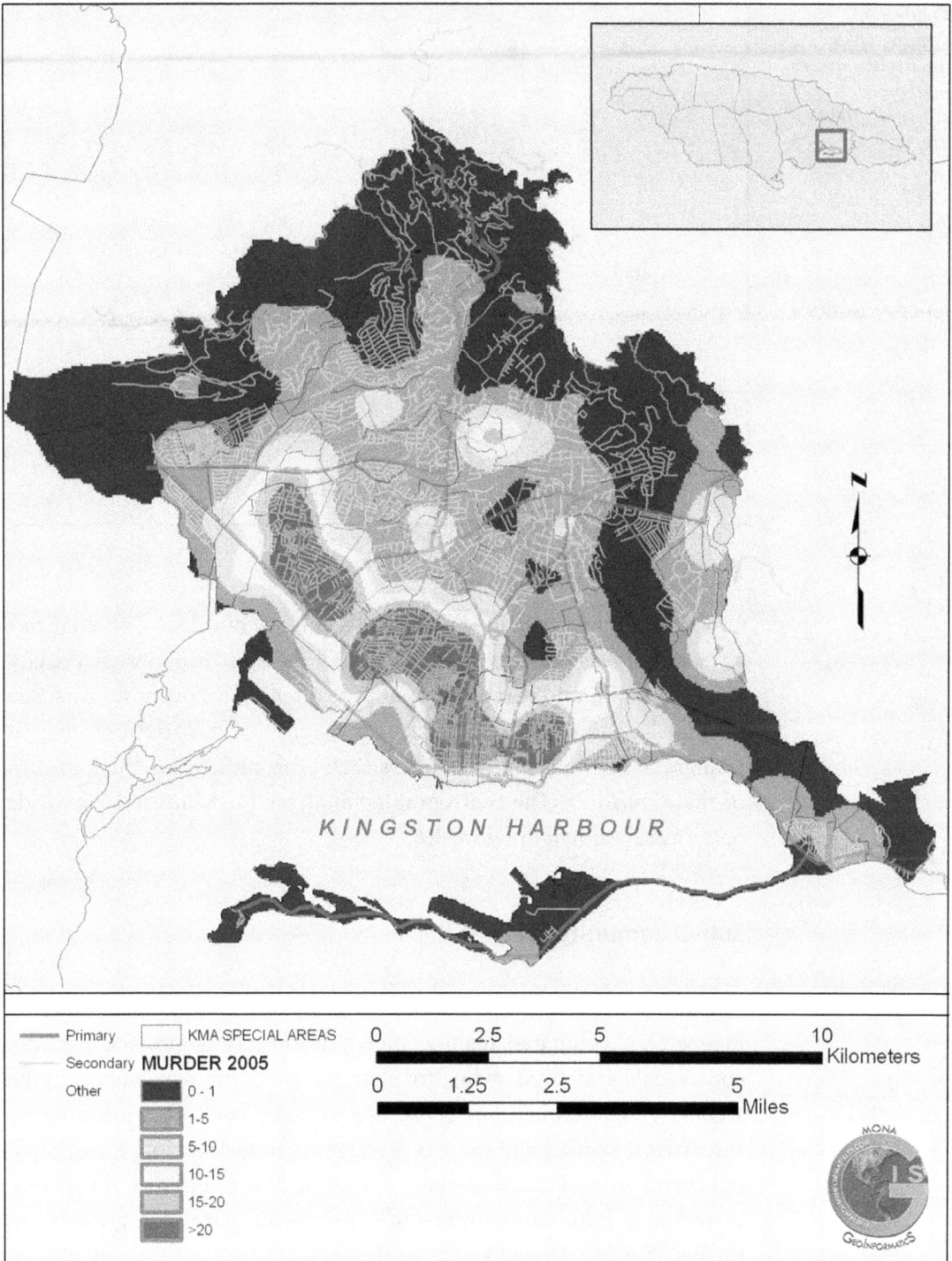

Figure 4.5 Murder hot-spot model of Kingston (2005)

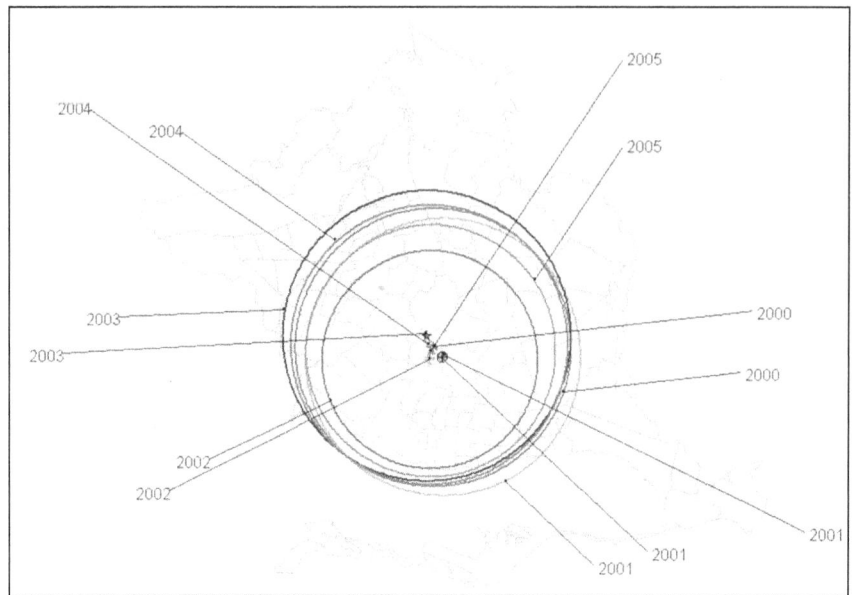

Cross Roads area remained the spatial centre of murders. This confirms a trend that was mostly visually observed: the murder pattern in the city is not random, and it repeats itself year after year. For most years, the standard distance is also fairly consistent, with variations due to changes in the numbers of murders each year, rather than the locations of these murders. The centrographic analyses for Kingston's homicide patterns are shown in figure 4.6.

Sub-Community Scale

At sub-community scale, individual assets in a community may be mapped and compared against crime locations. These provide a greater contextual detail by showing, for example, that crimes may occur in the vicinity of abandoned buildings, open lots or bars. This information can assist the police and security services in crime detection. It can guide policymakers and social workers as to how best to improve the quality of life of certain communities in order to mitigate high crime rates therein. Certain derelict buildings that may be havens for criminals can also be targeted for demolition.

Each "asset" in a community can be comprehensively mapped using GPS devices, and then classified and scored, ranging from low-risk assets (such as churches) to high-risk assets (such as abandoned buildings). These scorings can then be compared against different crime statistics, which can be similarly weighted: low-weight crimes may include loitering, moving up through medium-weight crimes (robberies, non-fatal violence-related injuries) to serious crimes (murders). The correlation between community assets and crime can guide the Jamaican police in responding optimally to rising crime. Figures 4.7 and 4.8 show community asset and crime models for the Kingston inner-city community of Rose Town.

Generally, the southern section of Rose Town is considered more crime prone than the north. Figures 4.7 and 4.8 show that this section also has relatively high concentrations of higher-risk assets, namely abandoned buildings.

If a correlation can be established between crime and the type of social assets present, then simulations can be run to determine the effect of the improvement or removal of the offending assets. This would lower the asset score for these areas, which could result in a lower crime score. The correlation at Rose Town was not particularly strong, and this modelling is now being attempted in other communities.

Operational Tools

Worldwide, many crime-fighting GIS programmes provide law enforcement agencies with operational tools to improve their abilities to respond to crime situations as well as plan their own resource deployment (for example, in Boston [Walter 2003] and Phoenix [Hill 2003]). These programmes are utilized within police departments as part of their in-house GIS units. GIS is therefore used in police operations planning (before, during and after operations) to coordinate exercises, manage personnel for staff training and development, and plan special events.

It is important that the police and security services have a very clear idea of the places they are expected to patrol and manage. The gathering of intelligence data (figure 4.9) is critical, as is the proper sharing of spatial information. GIS can be effectively utilized to generate and display this spatial information to illustrate the distribution of places of interest (a particular bar or club, for instance) in relation to roads and other features. As with the use of spatial tools for analytical purposes,

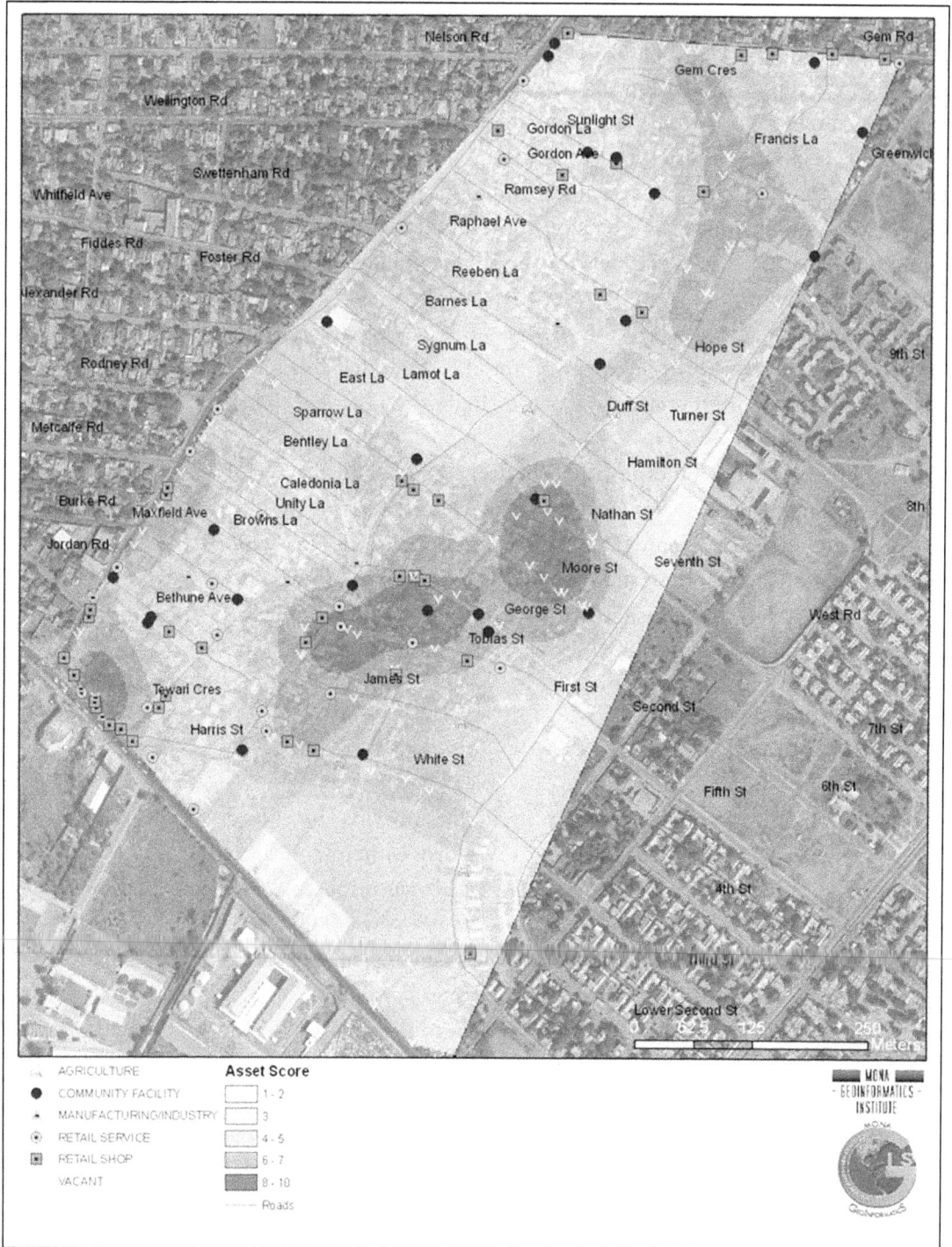

Figure 4.7 Weighted-asset model for Rose Town

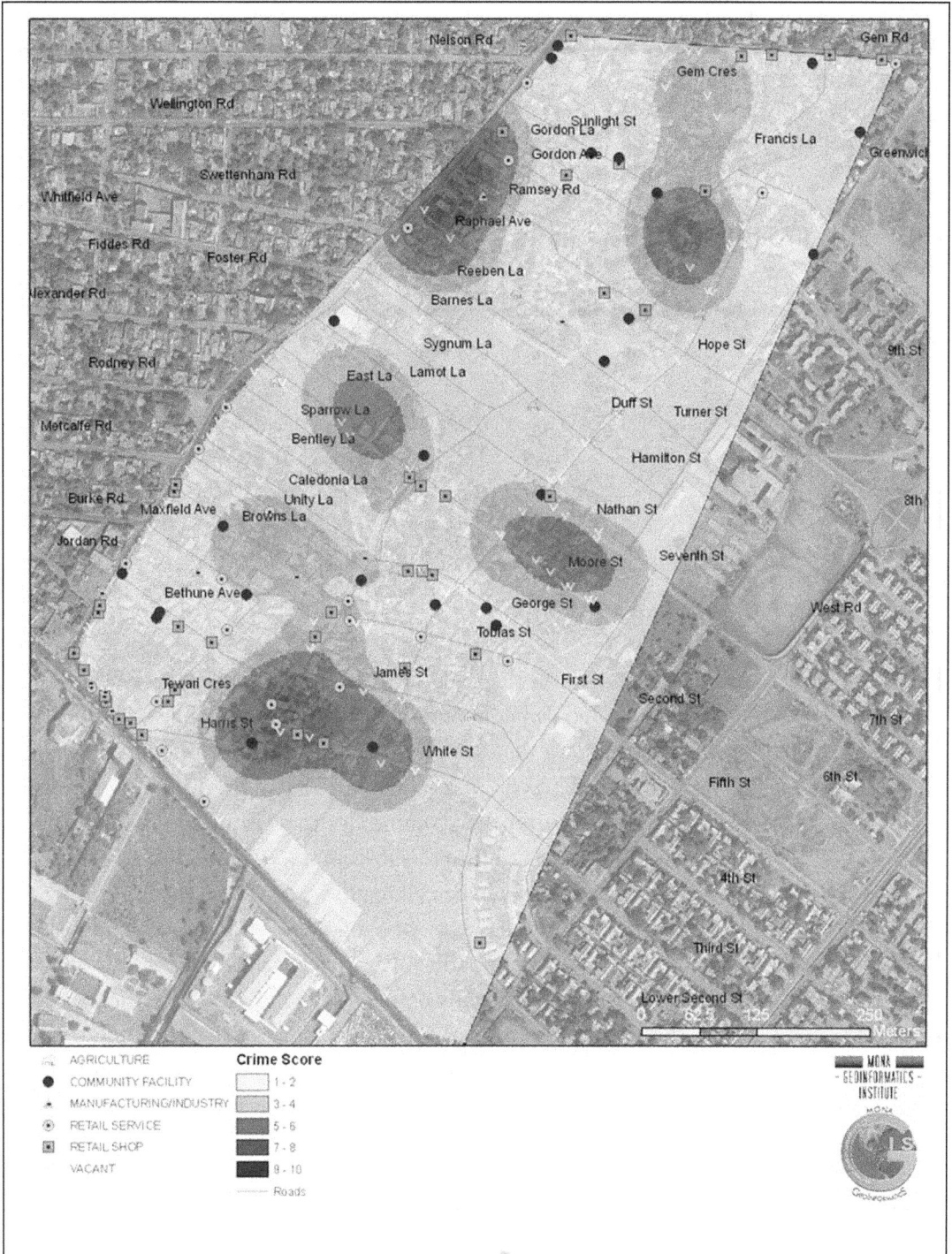

Figure 4.8 Weighted-crime model for Rose Town

Figure 4.9
Members of the Jamaica Constabulary Force using handheld GPS devices for intelligence gathering

this is dependent on the scale of use, as individual police stations will require more detailed community maps than entire police divisions.

Intelligence data that are plotted on detailed community maps may include mapped assets or features in the community, in addition to whole sections within that community that require particular police attention. In Jamaica, informal sub-community enclaves exist, and are generally referred to when describing the area. These enclaves, however, are often not clearly defined. Some of these areas (for example, areas called "Angola" or "Zimbabwe") may refer to gang territories or political garrisons, and are usually defined as being across a particular street or in the vicinity of an area. These boundaries are more random than geographic. Ground intelligence can help complete the definition of these places. Figure 4.10 is a police-division map for the Kingston Western Police Division showing enclaves within the division.

Once these maps containing both base data and police-specific information are created, either in hard copy or digital form, they can be used for pre-operations briefings and coordination of activities, as well as post-operations reviews. Commanders can use the maps to track the success or failure of the operations, and plan follow-up activities to update intelligence and other operational matters. The maps can also be

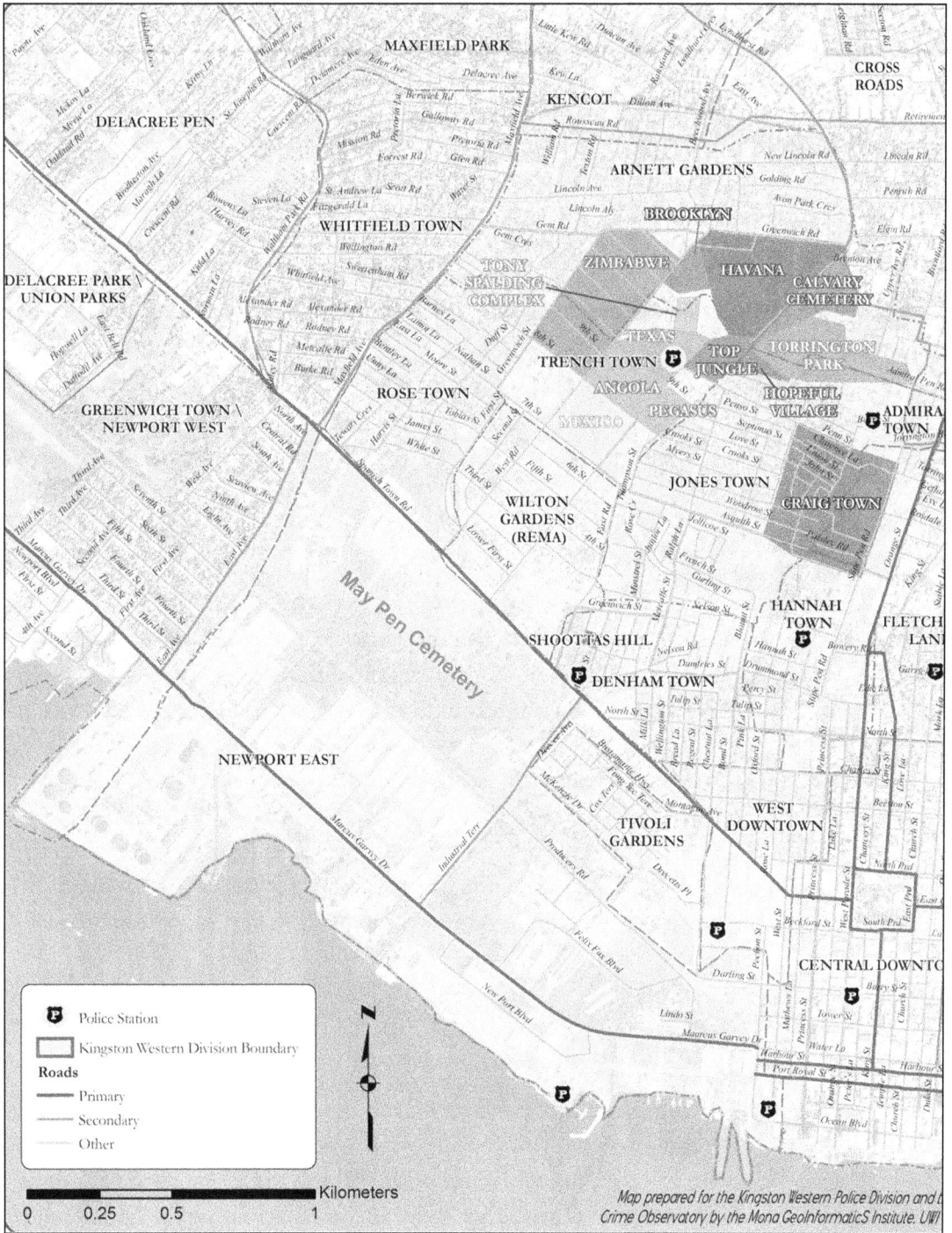

Figure 4.10 Divisional map of the Kingston Western Police Division

Figure 4.11
An example of an
operational use of
spatial tools for
crime fighting

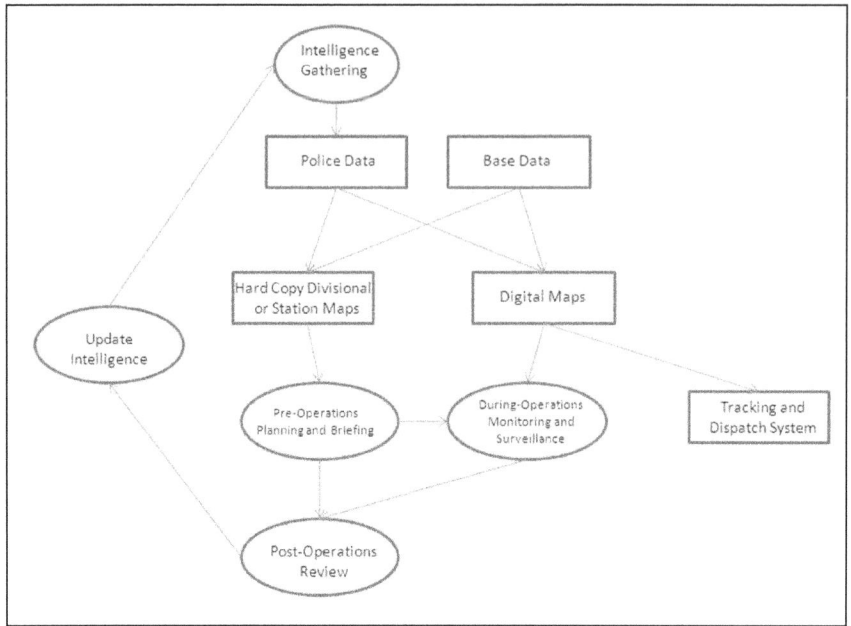

Figure 4.11
An example of an operational use of spatial tools for crime fighting

used to assist in resource management. GPS-enabled tracking of resources can be used in conjunction with the digital maps to monitor deployments, either in real time or *post facto*. This can be used to coordinate response (such as choosing the closest police unit to be deployed to respond to an emergency) or review present deployment. Similarly, the maps can also be used for training purposes, as well as for the planning of special events, for example, the opening of parliament, state functions, re-routing traffic for special sporting events and so on. Figure 4.11 provides a graphic representation of how spatial tools may be used in crime fighting.

Conclusions

The wide-scale deployment of a full suite of GIS and GIS-related tools for crime fighting will depend on the costs and utility of the system. It will not be exclusively police who will use these spatial tools, as non-police personnel will also have restricted access to the entire police database. It is clear that a mixed application of the spatial tools, for both analytical and operational uses, would be the most effective way of combating crime in Jamaica. A purely technological solution based on GIS technology will not accomplish anything if it is not subject to careful analyses relating to the social, economic and political contexts of crime in Jamaica. It must also be attended by mathematical analyses of the spatial patterns and the crime attributes that accompany crime locations. Used in conjunction with other approaches, GIS-based methods can provide the necessary tools to effectively tackle Jamaica's rising crime.

Acknowledgments

The author would like to acknowledge the assistance of Dr Elizabeth Ward from the Violence Prevention Alliance and the Crime Observatory for giving me the opportunity to apply geospatial tools with respect to the crime problem facing Jamaica. Special recognition also goes to Lisa-Gaye Webb of the Mona GeoInformatics Institute, as well as Professor Anthony Harriott (Department of Government, University of the West Indies, Mona), Bertrand Laurent (USAID), and Superintendent Anthony Morris, Superintendent Delroy Hewitt and Assistant Commissioner John McLean of the Jamaica Constabulary Force.

References

Harries, K. 1999. *Mapping Crime: Principle and Practice*. Washington, DC: National Institute of Justice, US Department of Justice.

Hill, B. 2003. Operationalizing GIS to Investigate Serial Robberies in Phoenix, Arizona. In *GIS in Law Enforcement: Implementation Issues and Case Studies*, ed. M.R. Leipnik and D.P. Albert. London: Taylor and Francis.

Lee, J., and D.W.S. Wong. 2001. *Statistical Analysis with ArcView GIS*. New York: John Wiley.

Lyew-Ayee, P. 2006. Crime Mapping, Analysis, and Strategies for Crime Mitigation. Special Report to the Ministry of Health/Health Promotion and Protection Division, Jamaica.

Statistical Institute of Jamaica. 2003a. *Population Census 2001 Jamaica, Volume 1: Country Report*. Kingston: Statistical Institute of Jamaica.

———. 2003b. *Population Census 2001 Jamaica*. Volume 2. *Age and Sex*. Kingston: Statistical Institute of Jamaica.

Walter, C. 2003. Crime Mapping at the Boston Police Department. In *GIS in Law Enforcement: Implementation Issues and Case Studies*, ed. M.R. Leipnik and D.P. Albert. London: Taylor and Francis.

5

Shoe-Print Identification

A Case Study from Grenada

TREVOR **MODESTE**

Although shoe-print identification is commonly used in both the United States and Europe in forensic investigations, it is not as commonly practised in the anglophone Caribbean. The case study of Regina versus Aldin Phillip *provides a good example of the use of shoe-print identification in the Caribbean. In 2000, Aldin Phillip and three other men robbed Paul (also known as Leon) and Mary Joseph of EC$30,000 in cash and EC$8,000 in jewellery. Shoe prints were found on the scene, an identification was made and a case presented in court. The methods and techniques used in the case will be presented in this chapter.*

Introduction

Shoe prints are found at scenes of crimes with great regularity. For this reason they have long been studied by police and crime laboratory personnel (Shoeprint and Footprint Comparisons n.d.). Shoe prints may be found as either prints or impressions. Prints are two-dimensional, made by depositing or removing material from a hard surface. Impressions are three-dimensional and made in a pliable material. Both class and individual characteristics are present in each of the two types of trace evidence and are identifiable. A shoe print is unique due to its many variables: length of wear, random marks and scratches, and the design on a particular sole. For prints, lifting with foil and photography is the major technique, and it is often combined with casting for impressions.

There is no doubt that a comparison of a shoe trace found at the scene of crime compared with prints obtained from a defendant can be valuable in associating the defendant with a crime. The difficult question to answer is whether a particular shoe trace can be positively identified as having been made by a specific item of footwear. Even though there is no recognized "science" of footwear comparisons, it has been widely accepted by US law enforcement as well as by the US courts that this kind of identification can be made when adequate evidence is available. It is not as commonly used as fingerprinting and other more traditional forensic science disciplines, because it is sometimes unreliable (Armstrong 2004). Despite this, the science of footwear investigations is evolving in the United States and Europe, as a growing body of research is being devoted to shoe-print identification (Armstrong 2004; Bowen and Schneider 2007; Shoeprint and Footprint Comparisons n.d.). In Europe, there are many specialists on footwear identification, and this technique is increasingly being applied in solving forensic cases. A study of several jurisdictions in Switzerland, for example, revealed that 35 per cent of crime scenes had shoe prints usable in forensic investigation. In both the United States and Europe, there are computerized shoe-print databases utilized by crime detectives (Geradts and Keijzer 1996; Mikkonen and Astikainenn 1994; Sawyer 1995). The following case study of *Regina versus Aldin Phillip* is a good example of shoe-print identification in the Caribbean. In 2000, Aldin Phillip and three other men robbed Mr Paul and Mary Joseph of EC$30,000 in cash and EC$8,000 in jewellery. Shoe prints were found on the scene, an identification was made and a case presented in court. The methods and techniques used in the case will be presented in this chapter. As the principal investigator, I will recount details of the case in the first person.

Presentation of the Case Itself

I arrived on the scene in Beaureguard about 7:30 a.m. on Monday, February 29, 2000. This was at the home of Paul and Mary Joseph, who owned a small wholesale business on the bottom floor of their house and reported a robbery of EC$21,200, US$10,055 and articles valued at EC$7,315. This robbery was consistent with recent robberies in which large sums of money were taken away.

The series of robberies started in November 1999. Some were committed at small business places, restaurants and gas stations, and no physical evidence was found at the scenes of the crimes. The suspects were always dressed in long coats, gloves and stocking masks, and they used a getaway vehicle. All the known robbers were checked out, those in prison and those out of prison. Deportees were also considered, and the name Aldin Phillip, alias "Ossie", came up.

He had been deported to Grenada from Trinidad in the month of November 1999 and was seen with some of the criminal elements in the Grand Anse area, south of the island, which is the main tourist belt. After living in Grenada for three months he bought a car for EC$20,000. Information revealed that he had never worked in Grenada and was deported from Trinidad penniless. "Ossie" was later detained for questioning in some summary incidents and was not under surveillance, but an alert was set up for him. Around the same time, guidelines were issued for dealing with crime scenes, and searching for footwear and footprints at all crime scenes became mandatory.

On the scene at Beauregard was an attachment of criminal investigation personnel from the Grenville Police Station headed by Sergeant Gill. They were in one section of the house with the occupants. All investigators were barefoot and wearing gloves. This was the procedure that had been adopted for all the recent robberies. I spoke to Sergeant Gill and commended him for his role in preserving the scene, and I commenced my examination. The building was a concrete structure; the storeroom was on the bottom floor and living quarters on the top floor. It comprised four bedrooms, two bathrooms, combined kitchen and living room, dining room, and an L-shaped verandah. I started dusting for fingerprints and footprints under the kitchen window on the southern side of the house, working from the outside and proceeding to the inside. I dusted on the cupboard under the window and a shoe print became visible. I then photographed and lifted the prints (see figure 5.1).

Processing of Footwear and Footprint Impressions

In order to process footwear and footprint impressions on hard, smooth, clean surfaces such as polished wood, tiles, glass and glazed floors the following steps should be taken:

1. Apply fingerprint powder to the surface by dusting with a fingerprint brush.

2. After an image is developed, place a rule or measuring device from toe to heel.

3. Enclose or circle the image with a grease pencil, placing date and initials alongside the image.

4. Photograph the image with the rule, date, and initials. During this exercise the camera should be placed on a levelled tripod.

5. Lift the prints with date and initials, and place them on footwear card backings.

6. Write on the back of the card a description of where the prints were found with time, date and initials.

The process for impressions on hard, smooth, dusty surfaces requires different steps.

1. Photograph impressions as they were.

2. Enclose impressions with grease pencil, and place date and initials alongside the image.

3. Photograph impressions by placing the camera on a tripod with level.

4. Lift the prints with the written information.

5. Apply fingerprint powder where prints were lifted.

6. Photograph, lift prints and place on footwear card backings.

7. Write on the back of the card a description of where the prints were found, along with date, time and initials.

Processing impressions on carpet or rugs involves the use of the electro-static footprints lifting machine. Here are the instructions:

1. Spread the collection sheet.

2. Connect the high voltage supply unit to the sheet.

3. Place the ground net about six inches away from the sheet.

4. Connect the ground wire to the high voltage supply and the ground net.

5. Set the charge by pushing the switch on the high voltage supply for seven to eight seconds.

6. Lift the collection sheet so the footprints or shoe prints will be visible.

7. Photograph and lift as above.

There are also specific steps to follow when processing shoe prints and footprints in soil:

1. Photograph the impression as it is and the general area.
2. Place the rule, date, identification and initial in soil.
3. Take close-up photographs by using oblique lighting from different angles and positions.
4. Make a cast using dental stone or plaster of Paris; write date and initials on cast while it is hardening.
5. Photograph before and after the cast is removed.

The best way to process a crime scene for footwear impression, on hard surfaces that have been stepped on, is with the use of fingerprint powder. These hard surfaces may be tiled floors or perhaps polished wood, glass or concrete, but the surfaces must be clean with no visible particles. The impressions may be latent or visible. The fingerprint powder will adhere to the areas where the shoe made contact with the surface. The powder should be applied by using a fingerprint brush, and a positive image of the outsole of the shoe will develop. The developed impression will be the mirror image of the shoe outsole. The print should then be photographed and lifted.

The impression is photographed by placing a rule alongside, writing with a grease pencil the date, the initials of the person who developed the prints, and, if possible, the complainant's initials. The impression should be enclosed or circled with the information written alongside the print. The camera should be on a tripod for balance and stability, and placed directly over the print. I like to use a flashlight at different angles to determine which angle is best suited to hold the electronic flash, or, alternatively, hold the electronic flash at a 45-degree angle to take the photograph. In this investigation I did not use a flash; the available lighting in the room was sufficient to photograph the print.

The pieces of equipment used at the Joseph's home were a 35-millimetre Nikon camera, a 52-millimetre lens, a ruler, a tripod, a level and a grease pencil. The tripod was placed over the print with the camera attached to it and the level was placed on the back of the camera to make sure that it was level and stable. The print was enclosed with the grease pencil, the date and my initials were written, and then the photograph was taken. To lift the print, fingerprint lifting tape and white, hard paper backing, or shoe-print backing, was used. The adhesive part was rubbed on the developed print and then peeled off and placed on the white paper backing. The location where the print was found, the date and my initials were written on the back of the card.

In the living room, four more shoe prints were found on the floor leading towards a bedroom. It appeared to be the first bedroom the robbers went to when they entered the house. The prints found on the floor were different to those found on the cupboard. Also observed were barefoot prints, but they were not documented based on the information given by Mrs Joseph. The shoe prints were photographed and lifted in the same manner as mentioned above.

Mrs Joseph said that she was not asleep. She saw someone in the doorway of her bedroom, who she thought was her son, and called out to him three times. When he did not answer, she woke her husband.

> They could not see us where we were because the room was dark and we were not on the bed. So it was when my husband got up they realized where we were and they came into the room. One held on to me and placed a gun to the back of my head; one held on to Leon [Paul] and placed a gun at his head and the other asked where we had the money. Leon told them that it was in the clothes closet. Leon put on the light when they went to the closet and I saw that the one who asked for the money had on an expensive sneaker.

The next day Sergeant Toussaint informed me that, on the night of the robbery, she had seen Aldin Phillip in Sauteurs, and he was spending US money. That gave us a lead in the investigation. It was now a matter of picking up the suspect. The following day, he was picked up by the Drug Squad for driving without a driver's licence and was brought to the Criminal Investigation Department. He was relieved of his sneakers by A.S.P. Maitland, who handed them to me in the presence of the suspect. I told him that the outsole resembled prints that were found at the home of Mr and Mrs Joseph in Beaureguard, St Andrew's after a robbery. A.S.P. Maitland then placed his initials on the shoes and I did the same, but Aldin Phillip refused when requested to do likewise.

I took the sneakers to my office where I made an impression of the outsole by greasing the sole of the right shoe with Vaseline, then stepping on to a white piece of paper and dusting the paper with fingerprint powder. The print developed was compared to the prints I found at the crime scene and there was a match. I found that the prints of Phillip's shoes were the same size, shape and design as the prints found in the

house of Mr and Mrs Joseph. They were also identical in class characteristics. Further examination revealed that there were three accidental
characteristics on the outsole of the shoes. One was a wearing-away
and a split in the rubber that could have been caused by a hard object
like a stone or piece of concrete, the second was a break in the ridge of
the design, and the last was the breaking away of the manufacturer's
number and logo under the shoes. The investigators were then informed
of my findings.

Making the Identification

The importance of class and accidental characteristics (individual or
identifying) in footwear identification cannot be overemphasized. To
recognize, retrieve, protect, analyse and place a value to the characteristics in a case is of paramount importance. A class characteristic places
the shoe in a common group, like same size, shape, style, pattern and
model. In the manufacturing of a shoe there may be some features that
repeat in other shoes that came from the same mould. These characteristics can be caused by objects or dust in the mould and are very prevalent in rubber sole shoes. In the mould itself faults may occur due to the
hand-held steel die which is used to mark or make the design or pattern
of the outsoles. They are all class characteristics, but can also be termed
identifiable features in that class.

The accidental characteristics are the individual or identifying features that are caused due to the wear and tear of the outsole of a shoe.
These characteristics cannot be duplicated in another shoe, even one of
the same exact size, shape, depth or position. They are caused by occu-
pational hazards – wear pattern, abrasion on contact with hard surfaces, cuts and nicks from sharp objects and air bubbles in their
manufacturing. These characteristics occur randomly on the outsoles of
shoes. The value of these characteristics is the nature of the wide range
of chance occurrence; they are individual characteristics that occur by
chance and not in a set or organized manner as the class characteristics.
They are of different size, depth, shape and length, and are the individual and identifying characteristics that are used to identify footwear.

Identification can be made whenever there are a sufficient number of
characteristics in the questioned or crime-scene impression that corre-
spond with the known shoe impression. The control mechanisms that

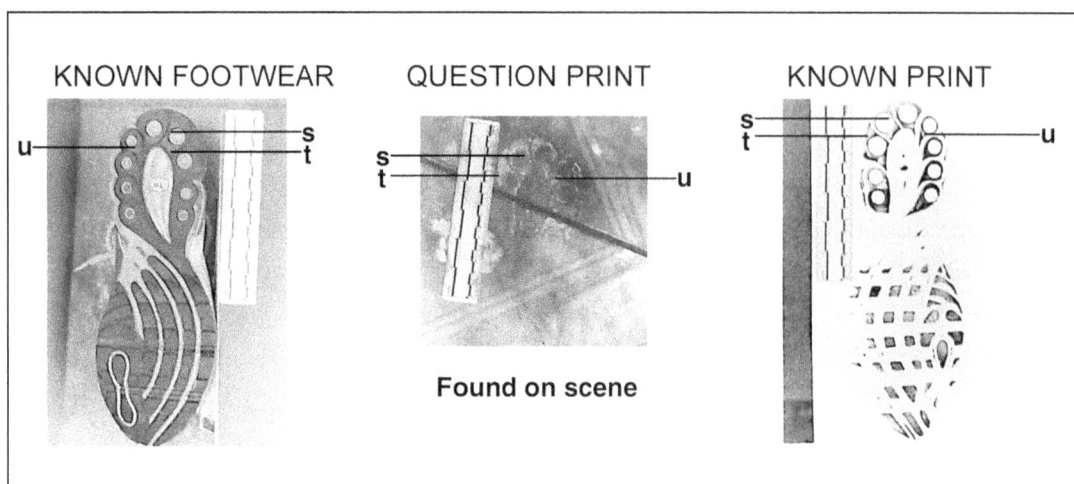

KNOWN FOOTWEAR **QUESTION PRINT** **KNOWN PRINT**

Found on scene

Figure 5.1
Chart prepared
and presented in
the Regina Phillip
case

the expert can use as it relates to the individual characteristics are as follows: clarity of the characteristics, uniqueness, reproducibility and randomness. For the class characteristics, the control mechanism mechanics are whether the prints are an exact match, the same length, width, size and side, and whether it is a perfect superimposition with the individual characteristic covering each other and the same distances apart.

To illustrate the identification, a chart or other medium has to be made to identify, highlight and point out the accidental characteristics. These characteristics can be any number, but the uniqueness, clarity and ability to be reproduced have to be taken into consideration. Photographic enlargements have to be made of the known impression, the known shoes and the questioned impression, then placed side by side and the characteristics identified and pointed out. The photographs should be taken with a ruler so that in the printing, they can be enlarged to the same size. The questioned impression should be placed in the centre, the known shoe to the left and the known impression to the right. The characteristics can be pointed out with lines and marked with letters or figures as shown in figure 5.1 above.

The Courtroom

Before I could give any evidence on footwear identification, I first have to be accepted as an expert and clarify my statements concerning footwear identification. This is done in a *voir dire* (trial within a trial), which begins like this:

> My name is Trevor Modeste. I am a police inspector attached to the Criminal Records Office. My duties at the CRO include photography; bloodstain pattern interpretation; fingerprint identification; footwear and tire thread identification; crime-scene investigation, and chart and cast preparation. I have been attached to the Criminal Records Office for the past eighteen years and I have been actively engaged in the above-mentioned fields.

Then I was led into evidence regarding my training in that field. I listed my training, starting in 1980 at the Captain St Louis Police Academy in Havana, Cuba, where I did specialist courses in Criminal Identification, including footwear identification. I then proceeded to the Royal Canadian Mounted Police College in Ottawa, Canada, and concluded my training at the Metro Dade Police institution in Miami Dade, Florida, doing digital photography in 2006.

A curriculum vitae can also be handed to the defence before the trial begins, and they may ask for a conference if they accept your training and qualification. This will make things easier for the expert, in some cases, but it is best to disclose your credentials to the court, since this can have a positive impact on the jury and will put them in a better position to make a general assessment of your qualifications, training and experience.

One can be very brief or very detailed when giving this information, using a variety of formats or styles. When giving dates, you may either begin from the furthest date to the most recent, or vice versa. You can similarly alter the chronology of institutions that you attended, but the field in which you are qualifying must be highlighted. Thus, in footwear evidence, footwear identification is the field in which emphasis must be placed.

The defence will then have the opportunity to challenge your credentials. Their duty is to make sure that you are not deemed an expert by the court, or that too much credibility be placed on your evidence as an expert. The defence will try to make it appear that you are not qualified to give that type of evidence; they will try to ridicule and insult you, but that is their job. I view it as a show that has to be performed by the defence and nothing more, because you will be accepted by the court in the end. It is only the judge who has to be satisfied that you have more training and experience in your stated field than the average person, and you will help the court to form an opinion it cannot form on its own. An expert witness is someone who has education or special training, skill or experience in a subject area to a greater extent than the average person. It is his or her duty to assist the judge and jury in understanding complicated things in that field. If the judge sees you as such a person and deems you to be an expert witness, you then go on to qualify the subject area.

Footwear identification is a well-known field in criminal identification. It is part of the science of criminalistics and is practised by police in countries like England, Canada and the United States. It is just as reliable as other means of criminal identification even though it is not as well known as the science of fingerprinting. In England, it is recognized and accepted that shoe-print evidence or footprint evidence is admissible and is by itself enough for a conviction. Convictions on that type of evidence are upheld on appeal.

In Grenada, I have made identifications with footwear impressions, but never had the opportunity to testify at the highest level of the court system because the suspects have pleaded guilty. There are currently two pending cases in the magistrate's court and another in the high court.

The above outlines the essential part of my qualifications. After this was presented to the court, I started giving my evidence.

The facts had to be established that I visited the scene of the robbery at the home of Mr Paul and Mrs Mary Joseph in Beaureguard, St Andrew's. It also had to be established that the examinations were carried out on the scene, in whose presence, how the shoe came into my possession and what I did with it.

Interpreting the facts or putting together the data will justify my opinion. To successfully demonstrate to the court my findings, the use of enlarged photographs or charts have to be presented. This acts as an effective technique that will capture the interest of the jury and they will more easily see and follow how I came to my opinion. These illustrations will aid in testifying and the jury will have them to review when they retire to consider the evidence. As shown above, the charts should be clearly labelled, the characteristics clear and pointed out on the enlargements.

The Probability Theory in Footwear Identification

The prosecutor may ask what is the probability of a characteristic repeating itself in another impression. I try to stay away from numbers in my answers, but if I am pressed to give the numerical probability answer then I would say that probability is the number of times an event can occur divided by the number of times which it cannot occur plus the number of times in which it can occur.

In other words, put nine different fruit in a box: apple, mango, grape, pear, banana, orange, plum, tamarind and damsel. The number of times the orange can be retrieved is once. The number of times it cannot be retrieved is eight. Add this number to the number of times it cannot be retrieved: one. This gives you a probability of one to nine that you will retrieve an orange.

Depending on the size of the shoe and also the size of the characteristic, one can come up with more difficulties of characteristic repeating. Now, if it is a size ten shoe and the outsole is measured at 9,000 square millimetres and the characteristic is smaller than a square millimetre, the answer will be a probability of 1 to 9,000 of the pattern repeating itself. This is a simple answer where the size, location, depth and shape are not taken into consideration, so the probability would move to the millions if they are taken into account. Then it was the question of my opinion.

In this case I stated, based on my findings as illustrated by the chart, it is my opinion that the impression found on the crime scene in Beaureguard, St Andrew's, at the home of the Josephs, and the impression I made from the right sneaker that was handed to me by A.S.P. Maitland were made by the same shoe.

Here the defence may cross-examine, object or make a submission. In this case, they objected to the admissibility of certain items relating to shoe-print evidence. The objection and the ruling are set out here.

Ruling on the Admissibility of Shoe-Print Evidence

Regina versus Aldin Phillip ruling on the admissibility of shoe-print evidence was delivered on March 26, 2001. Appearing for the prosecution were Mr H. Wildman and Mr J. Tyme and for the accused, Mr A. Clouden.

[1] FARARA, J. Learned Counsel for the accused objected to the admissibility of certain items relating to shoe-print evidence by the witness Inspector Trevor Modeste. These include a chart prepared by the witness, displaying the shoe print lifted at the scene of the crime, the right shoe taken from the foot of the accused at the Central Police Station by A.S.P. Maitland on 2nd March 2000, with the cooperation of the accused, and a print made from that shoe.

[2] The pair of sneakers taken from the feet of the accused by A.S.P. Maitland and handed over to Inspector Modeste on 2nd March, 2000 had been previously admitted without objection, as Exhibit "R.M.1".

[3] The witness Inspector Modeste has given evidence as to his training and experience in the field of shoe-print identification and other forensic skills, going back to 1985. He was accepted as an expert in this field without objection.

[4] Counsel for the accused submitted, in the main, that the Court has an overriding discretion not to admit evidence where the prejudicial value outweighs its probative value, or where that evidence was obtained by unfair means – the "fairness rule". In this regard, he relied on the statements of Lord Lane, C.J. in Quinn [1990] Crim. L.R. 581 as follows:

> "The function of the judge is therefore *to protect the fairness of the proceedings*, and normally proceedings are fair if a jury hears *all relevant* evidence which either side wishes to place before it, but proceedings may become unfair if, for example, one side is allowed to adduce relevant evidence which, for one reason or another, the other side cannot properly challenge or meet, or where there has been an abuse of process, e.g., because evidence has been obtained in deliberate breach of procedures laid down in an official code of practice."

[5] Mr Clouden submitted that the burden of proof remains on the Prosecution. With this no one can take issue. It is the Prosecution who must satisfy the Court as to the admissibility of the evidence, the subject matter of the objection.

[6] Mr Clouden contends that there is no evidence before the Court where a comparison was made with respect to shoes taken from the home of the accused, and that taken from his feet at the Central Police Station whilst in custody, including such comparisons relative to his shoe size and the like. He said this is important especially where the accused said to A.S.P. Maitland that he had borrowed the pair of sneakers taken from a prisoner in the cells at the Central Police Station, and where the only evidence in this case to connect the accused with the crime are those shoes, which were not found at the crime scene.

[7] Mr Clouden further submits that the Court, in exercising its discretion whether to exclude this evidence, should take cognizance of the fact

that the shoe in question was obtained by the police some 2 to 3 days after the commission of the alleged offence and would have necessarily been worn during that period; that Inspector Modeste is a Police Officer testifying on behalf of the State and, as such, is not an independent expert witness.

[8]   He also contends that shoe-print evidence is less reliable than fingerprint or palm print evidence, and must be looked at more closely. In short, Mr Clouden concluded that the prejudicial effect of this evidence outweighs its probative value and it would be unfair to the accused, who, because of lack of sufficient financial resources, has been unable to obtain his own expert opinion on this aspect of the evidence, to admit the evidence in question.

[9]   Learned Counsel for the Prosecution, Mr Wildman submitted:
(1)   the evidence in question is essentially a question of fact for the jury;
(2)   the fact that there is no other expert evidence that the Defence is able to produce in no way affects the admissibility of the evidence and there is no such rule of law or evidence;
(3)   invariably it is the Prosecution which puts on this type of evidence in criminal cases;
(4)   the authorities such as *R v Sang* and *R v Celeste and Quinn* show that evidence of this nature is generally admissible, subject to the Court's discretion to exclude it in exceptional circumstances warranting its exclusion;
(5)   there is nothing put forward by the Defence which would warrant the Court exercising its discretion to exclude this evidence;
(6)   by section 167 of the Evidence Act Cap. 92 of Grenada and the Privy Counsel decision in *Eversley Thompson V R* [1998] 2 W.L.R. 927 English law relating to the admissibility or sufficiency of evidence is part of the Laws of Grenada;
(7)   in England it is generally recognized and accepted that shoe- print evidence or footprint evidence is admissible and is enough to ground a conviction. The Prosecutor cited *R v Mathew Christopher*, a 1998 decision of the English Court of Appeal, where the evidence from a crime scene was used to convict for murder. The conviction was upheld on appeal;
(8)   in the Canadian case of *R v Arcuri* (a 1998 decision at first instance) expert evidence regarding shoe prints found at the crime scene was accepted to ground a conviction for first degree murder. There the expert evidence was given by a qualified police officer;
(9)   that the three accidental characteristics found by Inspector Modeste are the distinguishing features which show that no other shoe could have made the shoe print found at the scene; and
(10) all of the criteria for admissibility set out in *R v Arcuri* have been amply met by the Prosecution in the evidence adduced thus far in this case.

[10] By virtue of section 167 of the Evidence Act Cap. 92 of Grenada the law and procedure in England relative to the admissibility and sufficiency of any evidence including documentary evidence applies in or is incorporated as part of the Laws of Grenada. (*See Eversley Thompson v R [1998] 2 W.L.R., 927.*)

[11] In England, as illustrated by the case of *R v Mathew Christopher* [a 1998 decision] footprint evidence, that is, evidence of footprints found at or near the crime scene are admissible in criminal proceedings. *See also Phipson on Evidence 5th Edition para 14–31*, where it is stated:

> "Fingerprints or foot marks of a defendant found near the scene of a crime are admissible."

[12] It follows therefore that in Grenada footprint or shoe-print evidence found at or near the scene of a crime is admissible to prove the identity of the perpetrator or perpetrators of the crime.

[13] Similarly, such evidence has been held admissible in Canada.

[14] In *R v Mc Donald* [1982] 52 N.S.R. (2d) 372, the Nova Scotia Court of Appeal dismissed an appeal against the decision of the trial judge that he was satisfied on the circumstantial evidence that the sneaker of the accused was involved in the crime. In that case, a corporal of the Royal Canadian Mounted Police had testified that he had compared a footprint impression made by a sneaker taken from the accused, with a footprint impression taken the day before from a piece of broken glass window at the scene of the crime. His opinion was that the impression on the glass was made by the accused's sneaker, having observed more than 30 accidental characteristics between the two impressions, and that the statistical probability of two sneakers having the same accidental characteristics are in excess of one in ten million.

[15] Similarly, in *R v Daucette* [1992] N.S.J. No. 597, the Nova Scotia Provincial Court dealt with a criminal case involving an accused, who was found wearing shoes the day after the alleged offence, which were found to match a distinctive footprint found at the crime scene. The Court held that the taking of the accused's shoes with his cooperation was simply good police work and the shoes were essential to the investigation and conviction. It established the presence of the accused at the crime scene.

[16] In *R v Arcuri* the accused who was charged with murder voluntarily provided impressions of his inked bare feet on a sheet of paper which were then compared by an expert with impressions found and recovered from the scene. The judge found that the officer, who had been trained and experienced in the field of identifying print impressions, was a leader in that field. His evidence was reliable, clearly relevant and likely to assist the trier of fact. In that case, the judge at paragraph

17 of the judgment stated:

"Admission of expert evidence depends on the application of the following criteria:

(a) Relevance;

(b) Necessity in assisting the trier of fact;

(c) The absence of any exclusionary rule;

(d) A properly qualified expert."

[18] In the instant matter the witness, Inspector Modeste, had been accepted by the Court (without objection from Counsel for the accused) as an expert witness in the field of shoe-print evidence. He is, clearly from his training, including advanced training and experience in this field.

[19] The evidence, including the documents sought to be admitted into evidence by the Prosecution, are clearly relevant, as evidence which would tend to place the accused man at the scene of the crime at the relevant time.

[20] I am also satisfied that such evidence and documents will assist the jury as the trier of the facts in this case.

[21] In my view, there exists no exclusionary rule in Grenada (or England for that matter) which would operate to exclude the admission into evidence of this type of evidence. In this regard, one is not referring to the genial discretion of the Court to exclude evidence where its prejudicial effect outweighs its probative value or where it would inherently be unfair to allow the evidence.

[22] I am not satisfied as Counsel for the accused contends, that any matter concerning the collection and preservation of this evidence by Inspector Modeste or the obtaining of the pair of sneakers exhibit "R.M.1" by A.S.P. Maitland, would constitute grounds for the Court exercising its discretion to exclude the evidence.

[23] In my view, the evidence given by Inspector Modeste as to how this evidence was obtained and tested is sufficient to satisfy any test as to the reliability of that evidence.

[24] Matters such as whether the pair of sneakers "R.M.1" belonged to the accused, he having been wearing them on 2nd March, 2000 at Central Police Station, is for the triers of fact, the jury.

[25] Likewise, whether Inspector Modeste's expert opinion regarding the comparison and match of the right sneaker "R.M.1" with the shoe print lifted by him from the crime scene on 28th February, 2000 is to be accepted, is a matter for the jury. This issue and the reliability of his evidence is not adversely affected by the absence of any other expert evidence on that issue in the case.

[26] I therefore rule that the chart and other documents identified by the witness Inspector Modeste relative to shoe prints found at the crime scene and to the pair of sneakers Exhibit "R.M.1" are admitted into evidence and marked "Exhibit T.M.1".

Two more witnesses gave their testimony, the prosecution and defence addressed the jury, and the case was summed up by the judge. Then, the jury retired to consider the evidence. They returned with a guilty verdict in less than forty-five minutes.

References

Armstrong, Erin Daigh. 2004. Can Shoes Catch a Culprit? Or Does a Shoeprint Lie? *United States v. Allen*, 390 F.3d. http://forensic-evidence.com/site/ID/Shoeprint.html (accessed February 5, 2008).

Bowen, Robin, and Jessica Schneider. 2007. Forensic Databases: Paint, Shoe Prints, and Beyond. *National Institute of Justice Journal* 258 (October). http://www.ojp.usdoj.gov/nij/journals/258/forensic-databases.html (accessed February 5, 2008).

Geradts, Z., and J. Keijzer. 1996. The Image-Database REBEZO for Shoeprints with Developments on Automatic Classification of Shoe Designs. *Forensic Science International* 82 (1): 21–31.

Mikkonen, S., and T. Astikainenn. 1994. Databased Classification System for Shoe Sole Pattern: Identification of Partial Footwear Impression Found at a Scene of a Crime. *Journal of Forensic Science* 39 (5): 1227–36.

Sawyer, N. 1995. SHOE-FIT: A Computerised Shoe Print Database. In *Proceedings of the European Convention on Security and Detection*, 86–89. Brighton. http://ieeexplore.ieee.org/xpl/freeabs_all.jsp?arnumber=491545 (accessed February 5, 2008).

Shoeprint and Footprint Comparisons. N.d. http://forensic.to/shoeprint.html (accessed February 5, 2008).

6

An Unusual Case of Suicide

CARL MARTIN **WINSKOG**

An unusual case of suicidal hanging is described. A seventy-one-year-old Swedish male, with cancer of the lip and tongue, decided to take his own life. His decapitated body was found incidentally beneath a tree and his head separately about 4 metres away. At a height of 345 centimetres above the ground, a nylon rope was attached to a branch. Calculation of forces showed that, assuming he was standing on the branch when stepping out into the air, there would be sufficient energy from acceleration to achieve complete decapitation. This Swedish case study can be a useful frame of reference for studying hanging suicides in the Caribbean.

Introduction

Hanging is not a rare method of suicide in the Caribbean. In Barbados, hanging occurs only slightly less frequently than ingesting pesticide. The suicide rate in Trinidad and Tobago is much greater than that of its English-speaking Caribbean neighbours (Hutchinson et al. 1999). Many of these suicides are Paraquat induced. Paraquat is a standard herbicide used to kill various types of crops. The product causes lung damage if smoke from the crop is inhaled. Of 48 cases of suicide for 1996, 39 (81.3 per cent) were due to pesticide poisoning. Of the 1,133 suicides that occurred in Trinidad and Tobago from 1991 to 2000, 64.2 per cent were due to poisoning, 30.3 per cent to hanging, and 4.5 were due to other causes, including jumping from heights, self-wounding and firearms (Hutchinson 2005). Individuals of East Indian origin accounted for 89 per cent of the suicide victims (Hutchinson et al. 1999). Despite this, media reports from the twin island republic suggest that hanging is a fairly common suicide method. Guyana also suffers from a very high suicide rate, which is estimated at 27.2 people for each 100,000 people each year. Jamaica has also had its fair share of hanging suicides.

This following case study from Sweden can be used as a useful frame of reference for studying hanging suicides in the Caribbean. It is important to note that the suicide rate in Sweden is much higher than that of any country in the Caribbean. Death by hanging is the most common method of suicide in Sweden. In 1996, 32 per cent of all suicides were by hanging. Substantially more males (35 per cent) than females (24 per cent) prefer hanging in Sweden. And, among men suicide is the most common cause of death between the ages of fifteen to forty-four (National Board of Health and Welfare, Centre for Epidemiology, Stockholm 1998). Knowledge of a country's specific suicide culture and the epidemiology of suicide is important for an accurate interpretation of post-mortem findings.

Mechanisms

The mechanisms leading to death by hanging are different depending on the force applied and the location of the pressure on the neck, but the most common cause of death is the occlusion of the carotid arteries. Although it is commonly believed that a fracture of the cervical column is a common mechanism in hanging, this is hardly the case in reality. While the physiological cause of death in hanging is usually hard to determine, the mechanisms that eventually cause the individual to die can be divided into four groups (Raja and Sivaloganathan 1997; Hartshorne and Reay 1993; Vanesis 1989):

1. Stretching of the sinus carotis body, inducing a reflex with cardiac stop or arrhythmia
2. Occlusion of the major blood vessels in the neck
3. Occlusion of the airways in the neck
4. Stretching of the brain stem

In the following case report we present a rare case study, which involved a complete decapitation.

Background

In England during the seventeenth century, decapitation was a common complication at public judicial hangings. Before hanging the individual, the length of the rope was so arranged that it depended on the weight of the body. The purpose of this was to ensure that the drop was of maximal length and that the head would not be separated from the body. The energy developed during the drop should be 1,700 joules, and this amount of energy will induce instant unconsciousness, fracture and/or dislocation of the cervical vertebrae with injuries to the spinal cord and/or stretching of the brain stem. A similar procedure is still being used in the United States (Nokes et al. 1999). Decapitation during hanging is rare, and Rotschild and Schneider (1998) present ten cases in a review article.

Case History

A few years ago, outside a small village in mid-Sweden, a headless body of a male was found by two young women horseback riding through a small forest on a Sunday morning. They immediately called the police, who quickly arrived at the scene where they found a body of an elderly male lying on his back (figure 6.1).

The clothes were in order, but the head was found lying on the ground, less than 5 metres away, separated from the body. The body lay beneath a large pine tree and a nylon rope had been tied around a branch located 345 centimetres above the ground level. A loop of a spliced nylon rope was hanging 159 centimetre above the ground (figure 6.2).

At first it was not believed that hanging could have been the cause of the decapitation because a pool of blood was

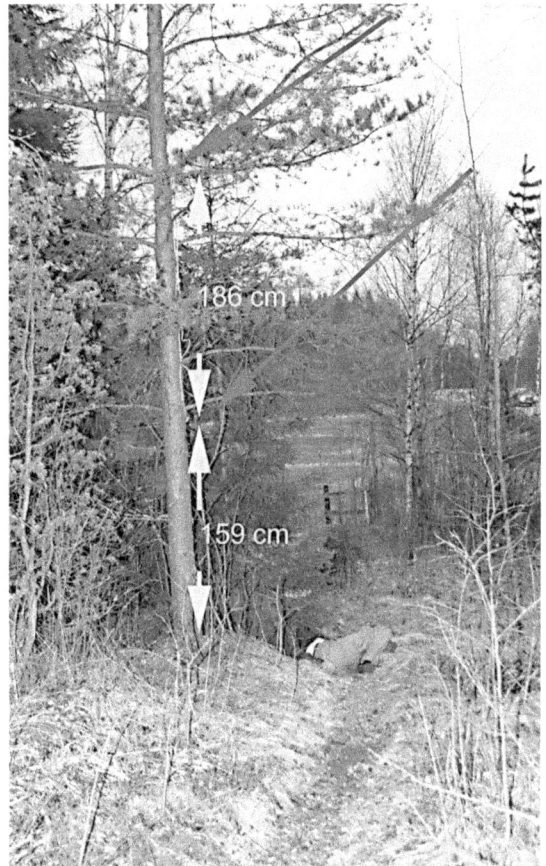

Figure 6.1 Body of an elderly male lying on his back

Figure 6.2 Nylon rope found hanging above the ground

Figure 6.3 Decapitated body

observed about one metre from the body, which gave the impression that the body had been moved after death. Moreover, a witness had observed a person walking in a hurry from the area. However, the man was soon identified, and it was established that he was not involved with the death of the old man. The dead body was later identified by documents found in his wallet. A suicide note was found. He was a seventy-one-year-old widower and was suffering from a lip cancer. He had difficulty eating due to a large opening in his lower lip. He suffered from chronic pain as well as social isolation. He described in his suicide letter that the lack of help and understanding from the healthcare system left him with no alternative but to take his own life.

The autopsy showed a male of 73.6 kilograms in weight and 187 centimetres in height. Despite his cancer, he appeared fit for his age. The decapitation wound was oriented horizontally just below the mandible (figure 6.3).

The edges of the wound displayed a circumferential skin abrasion varying between 0.2 and 1.0 centimetres, with a short interruption on the left side. The cervical column had been cut obliquely between the second and third cervical vertebras. The larynx was intact below the plane of decapitation. On the head side, a fractured hyoid bone and an uninjured tongue were seen. The other parts of the body showed no injuries. Microscopic examination revealed a growth of squamous epithelial cancer in the tongue and lower lip. Blood analysis of drugs and alcohol showed only ethanol in moderate concentrations, one per thousand.

Discussion

Complete decapitation by suicidal hanging has been described previously in about ten cases (Pankrantz et al. 1986; Raja and Sivaloganathan 1997; Tracqui et al. 1998; Rotschild and Schneider 1998). The case study in this chapter is similar to those cases in the following respects:

1. A ligature consisting of a running knot in a single loop was around the neck.
2. There was a strong twined rope.
3. A sharply defined, circular transsection was on the uppermost part of the neck.
4. A cervical fracture between C2 and C3 (in some cases the fracture was located between C1 and C2).

Both the weight of the body and drop heights are critical factors in judicial hangings. Tables were elaborated to avoid excessive force resulting in decapitation of the victim (Nokes et al. 1999). The biomechanical factors that separate the head from the rest of the body can be understood by calculating the energy (E) applied to the neck due to the body mass (m), the acceleration (g = 9.81m^2) and the distance(s) in a free fall. Other factors such as the rope, the circumference of the victim's neck, and the resistance of the skin and the soft tissues are therefore significant factors in the hangings.

In this case study, the distance in the free fall was calculated to be at least 343 centimetres. This would have resulted in an E = 3.43 x 9.81 x 73.6 = 2,477 kJ. The drop height was far above what would be regarded as optimal in a judicial hanging (Nokes et al. 1999). Even if the drop height in this case was overestimated by 100 centimetres, even that might have been sufficient to cause decapitation. The nylon rope was the kind normally used to tow cars. It was characterized by a high friction surface and low elasticity, that is, with a low ability to accumulate and disperse energy. The high friction around the neck would facilitate penetration through the skin by the relatively immobile surface of the loop. The circumference of the neck was not measured but it should influence the amount of energy per surface area.

Could the fact that this man suffered from cancer of the lip and tongue have influenced the tenacity of the tissues in the neck? The cancer was located on the tongue and the lower lip, and no signs of cancer could be seen in the edges of the decapitation wound. The muscles and soft tissue of the neck showed no signs of infiltration by the epithelial cancer.

Due to ignorance, this case was initially misdiagnosed as a homicide, given the rarity of decapitation in suicidal hanging in Sweden, even though the drop height of the hanging suicide clearly suggested suicide by decapitation. In other cases in which there are lower drop heights, other factors such as the quality of the rope and the victims' tissues should also be taken into consideration.

This case underscores the need for the forensic pathologist to accurately determine the kinds of suicides that are expected to occur in certain societies. A common method of suicide used in one place, or country, could be very rare in another. Knowledge about the different methods used in the community helps the forensic pathologist to differentiate an unusual case of suicide from what appears to be a normal case study. Forensic training, coupled with years of valuable work experience, are key in facilitating an accurate interpretation.

Acknowledgements

The images were published by the courtesy of Ragnar Nordanstig, Department of Criminalistics, Swedish Police Force, Karlstad, Sweden.

References

Hartshorne, Nikolas J., and Donald Reay. 1993. Letter to the Editor: Judicial Hanging. *American Journal for Forensic Medicine and Pathology* 16 (1): 87.

Hutchinson, G. 2005. Variation of Homicidal and Suicidal Behaviour within Trinidad and Tobago and the Associated Ecological Risk Factors. *West Indian Medical Journal* 54 (5): 319–24.

Hutchinson, G., H. Daisley, D. Simeon, V. Simmonds, M. Shetty and D. Lynn. 1999. High Rates of Paraquat-Induced Suicide in Southern Trinidad. *Suicide and Life Threatening Behavior* 29 (2): 186–91. New York: Guilford.

National Board of Health and Welfare, Centre for Epidemiology. 1998. *Statistics – Health and Diseases: Cause of Death 1996.* Stockholm: National Board of Health and Welfare.

Nokes, L.D.M., A. Roberts and D.S. James. 1999. Biomechanics of Judicial Hanging: A Case Report. *Medical, Science and the Law* 39 (1): 61–64.

Pankrantz, H., E. Schuller and E. Joseph. 1986. Dekapitation beim Erhängen. *Arch Kriminol* 178, nos. 5–6: 157–61.

Raja, U., and S. Sivaloganathan. 1997. Decapitation: A Rare Complication in Hanging. *Medical, Science and the Law* 37 (1): 81–83.

Rotschild, M.A., and V. Schneider. 1998. Decapitation as a Result of Suicidal Hanging. *Forensic Science International* 106 (1): 55–62.

Tracqui A., K. Fonmartin, A. Geraut, D. Pennera, S. Doray and B. Ludes. 1998. Suicidal Hanging Resulting in Complete Decapitation. *International Journal of Legal Medicine* 112: 55–57.

Vanesis, Peter. 1989. *Pathology of Neck Injury.* London: Butterworths.

7

The Case for Forensic Linguistics in Trinidad and Tobago

GODFREY A. **STEELE**

Forensic linguistics is the name given to the field of linguistics that concerns itself with the interface between language and the law. Forensic linguistics is a well-established discipline in the United Kingdom and the United States that focuses on civil and criminal applications, but its application in the Caribbean is relatively unknown. This chapter explores, through a survey of cases reported in the Trinidad and Tobago media, the possibilities for engaging forensic linguists in the finding of facts in selected cases. The selected cases deal with witness statements (involving changes to an original story, a disputed document, "suspicious evidence", a confession and the credibility of an unsigned witness statement). These examples have two main potential uses for forensic linguists in the Caribbean. They offer a model for defining the scope of forensic linguistics, including the boundaries that separate forensic fact-finding issues from legal issues. The cases also provide examples that could inform the development of a language and the law corpus for research.

Objectives

This chapter describes the scope of the field of forensic linguistics and explores its potential application in a Caribbean context. The chapter demonstrates how witness statements can be analysed using newspaper reports in the absence of original statements. Reported witness statements offer a valuable source for building a corpus for comparison with original statements and other versions when they are available.

Relevance to Judicial Outcomes

Since the forensic linguist can help legal officers to determine facts, and not the legality of witness statements, for example, forensic linguistic analysis can assist in determining authorship, authenticity and whether disputed texts (a confession, a report of a confession, or a written account of a witness statement, for example) are capable of being produced by the person attributed with authorship. A comparative analysis of lexical (word choice), syntactical (structure) and discourse elements (patterns of organizing text) provides a tool for comparing texts. Using a comparative analysis of direct speech newspaper accounts of what a witness said and the journalist's reported versions of what the witness said, it is possible to see how factual statements are represented in different ways. The different representations can have an impact on meaning, emphasis, and the establishment and interpretation of facts. The next stage is to obtain original transcripts or voice recordings when permission is granted. The writer of this chapter has sought permission to access the sources, but without success. In the absence of original sources, however, this chapter demonstrates that different versions exist in the reporting of witness statements. This demonstration supports the case for applying forensic linguistic analytical technology to assist judicial officers in fact finding, which ultimately can affect judicial outcomes.

Definition of Forensic Linguistics

Forensic linguistics is the name given to the field of linguistics that concerns itself with the interface between language and the law (Blackwell 2003). One of the professional associations for forensic linguistics has been described in this way, "The International Association of Forensic Linguists (IAFL) is an organization which primarily consists of linguists whose work involves them in the law. Narrowly defined, this means linguistic evidence in court (authorship attribution, disputed confessions etc.), but in fact the association aims to bring together those working on any aspects of language and the law" (IAFL 2006).

Forensic linguistics is a well-established discipline in the United Kingdom and the United States, albeit with different emphases on civil and criminal applications, but "the scope of the term 'forensic linguistics' remains somewhat vague" (Tiersma n.d.). Indeed, the term forensic linguist is controversial, as reflected in the following statement: "Although I believe that linguists can sometimes play an important role in helping a judge or jury decide both criminal and civil factual issues, I do not consider myself to be a forensic linguist. My interest is in the intersection and interaction of language and law. For my purposes, forensic linguistics, which strongly suggests helping solve criminal cases, is just too limited a term for what I do" (Tiersma n.d.). In contrast to the exclusive application of "forensic linguistics" to criminal matters, Tiersma offers an alternative definition that emphasizes fact-finding in criminal and civil matters.

> Thus, we can define forensic sciences more inclusively as encompassing any branch of scientific or technical expertise that is useful in deciding cases. It is important at this point to distinguish factual from legal issues. Judges and lawyers are the experts on the law, so they will almost invariably object if an expert in another field tries to opine on the meaning of a statute or judicial opinion. On the other hand, it is specifically the job of the jury (or, in a bench trial, of the judge) to decide questions of fact. The role of experts in the legal process is to assist the jury or judge (the "factfinder") to make all factual determinations. (Tiersma n.d.)

Forensic Linguistics within the Caribbean Context

In the Caribbean, the term forensic linguistics is relatively unknown. Although there are a few scholars working in this field, there remains the challenge of defining, articulating and applying forensic linguistics to the Caribbean language and law context. In particular, the language context of the Caribbean, and the challenges and realities of language use in a legal context, offer interesting and practical questions to linguists, as well as legal practitioners.

This chapter focuses on selected cases involving witness statements that may be of interest to the forensic linguist. The recording and use of witness statements has attracted the attention of forensic linguists elsewhere, but the potential application of forensic linguistics to criminal cases has not been frequently or widely reported in the Caribbean context or in the context of Caribbean linguistics. For example, cases involving the authenticity of the police record of interview in Australia have been described, but the linguist's expert evidence has not always been accepted, except on rare occasions (Eades 1994). Other situations include Dutch witness statements written by the police (Komter 2002), an analysis of the actual statement-taking process in the United Kingdom (Rock 2001) and the massaging of witness statements in Hong Kong (Tyrwhitt-Drake 2003).

A few scholars have reported on forensic linguistics witnesses in a Jamaican context or in a Jamaican Creole context. They include the encounter between Creole-speaking witness and English-speaking counsel (Forrester 2005), interaction patterns among judge, defence and prosecution counsels and witnesses (Shields- Brodber 2002), and a comparison of competing transcripts of Jamaican Creole in a murder case in New York (Patrick and Buell 2000). Evans (2005) has described the use of makeshift court interpreters in St Lucia. In the Trinidad context, there have been explorations of language and communication issues in the law (Steele 2005), and of possible course content in language and the law (Steele 2007). However, there are no known reports of forensic linguistic explorations of Trinidad and Tobago examples, except for a citation referring to the role of an interpreter who used Signed English with a deaf murder accused in Trinidad who understood American Sign Language and unknowingly pleaded guilty (Blackwell 2003; Marks 2003a, 2003b).

Forensic Linguistics within the Trinidad and Tobago Context

Using a few Trinidad and Tobago cases, this chapter makes the case for the application of forensic linguistics. It also makes the case for, in the absence of actual court transcripts, a collection of a corpus of newspaper reporting of witness statements. The newspaper reports can be compared with court transcripts or original recordings when they become available for research and analysis by forensic linguists interested in the recording and use of witness statements and courtroom language in a Caribbean language context. Although some newspaper reports can be potentially misleading or erroneous, they can be a rich source of data in comparing different versions of statements.

Witness Statements

State versus Bachan: *Changed Story*

An interesting area of forensic linguistics pertains to the witness statements or sometimes the statements of persons accused of a crime.

Often, authorship of the statement is disputed. Witnesses sometimes complain that the statement does not reflect what they said, or that someone changed what they had said. The language used in statements is referred to as "text" by some scholars, and as "spoken or written discourse" by others (Crystal 1997, 116). However, some authorities refer to such language as text when it represents what the speaker or writer produces, and discourse when there is interaction between two or more speakers/writers (Salkie 1995, xi). Often the language used in the statement is subject to scrutiny in so far as it helps to determine matters of fact, not legality. In the Dutch legal system, police transcripts of witnesses' (that is, suspects') own words are used by judges to ask suspects for confirmation of the information in the dossier (Komter 2002).

In example 1 cited below, Ramzan Bachan, who was jointly charged with the murder of a taxi driver, explains to the jury that he had changed his testimony because, sometime after he had given testimony, while praying, a voice told him to speak the truth (Ali 2006).

Example 1

"At first . . . I didn't expect nobody to believe my side of the story," Bachan told a jury, saying that he got scared after Joshua Ramnath and Daniel Goolcharan both struck agreements with the state to testify against him.

"About three days ago when I was saying my prayers, something tell me to talk the truth and the truth go set me free. If I is to go to the condemned [Death Row] and get my neck break [at least I know that] I talk the truth," he said.

In the example cited, matters relating to Bachan's motive(s) to change his mind, the admissibility of the statement or any legal issue do not fall within the expertise of the forensic linguist. Neither should the forensic linguist attempt to offer any advice in these matters. The job of the forensic linguist is to provide such assistance as may aid the jury in determining authorship, or to provide expert opinions based on any language evidence that may be adduced in order to make factual determinations about the disputed authorship of witness statements, for example. The job entails helping juries to make factual determinations rather than legal ones.

In criminal cases involving witness statements, the language attributed to the author sometimes appears not to be the language that the writer might produce independently of the person taking the statement. In the Bachan case, the journalist's reporting of the case (example 1A) presents what the witness said (example 1) to the jury in this way:

Example 1A

The Mayaro man on trial for murdering a taxi driver during a carjacking in 2001 claimed yesterday that it was one of his accomplices who killed the man and that he was unwittingly drawn into the crime. Bachan also admitted that he had changed his defence during the trial.

At first, he had insisted that he was not with Goolcharan and Ramanth [sic] when Elwyn Sampson was killed, but he eventually changed his story to put himself at the scene.

Lexical and syntactic analyses may be used to compare the journalist's words with the accused's words. For example, the journalist writes, "he eventually changed his story.", but the accused says, according to the journalist, "when I was saying my prayers, something tell me to tell the truth". The journalist also reports, "At first he had insisted that he was not with . . . but he eventually changed his story to put himself at the scene", but Bachan is reported to have said, " 'At first . . . I didn't expect nobody to believe my side of the story,' saying that he got scared after Ramnath and Goolcharan both struck agreements with the State to testify against him." Both the syntax and the word choices reflect different views of the situation. It would be interesting to compare the witness's oral statement to the jury with the written statements obtained by the police.

Often a statement is written and then signed by the person giving the statement after he or she has read it, if he or she can read, or after he or she has listened to it and accepted that the words captured what he or she had said. In the case of a Creole speaker, not only is there the issue of differences between spoken and written discourse, which is a valid issue for any speaker, but there is also the issue of the means by which spoken Creole may be compared with written Creole or some other written version of English. Newspaper reporting, court reporting and police recording of witness statements are not guaranteed to capture what the speaker said nor what version of the language was used. For instance, it would be interesting to compare the original statement given to the police by Bachan with the one in which "he eventually changed his story to put himself at the scene". A comparison of the discoursal features of both texts could establish discourse elements attributable to the same known author, or the author of disputed texts.

What happens when two versions of a statement are disputed? The discourse features identified in a case such as Bachan's could provide a baseline model in a database or corpus of witness statements. Some of the identifiable features include a comparison between the language of the witness's statement to the jury and the language of the original and revised statements. It would also be interesting to compare the journalist's version, which reported that Bachan "eventually changed his story to put himself at the scene", with Bachan's oral version in which he is reported by the journalist to have said to the jury "something tell me to talk the truth and the truth go set me free". We see, in example 1B, that later the reporter states the following:

Example 1B

Joshua Ramnath claimed he saw Bachan slit Sampson's throat with a knife, while Goolcharan testified that he did not see the killing.

Aaron Ramnath and his father, Vinoo Ramnath, testified that when the three got back after the robbery, they were tending to cuts Bachan and Goolcharan received when Bachan said he "buss a man throat".

Bachan testified yesterday that the trip to El Socorro was his first time leaving Ortoire/Mayaro, and he went with Goolcharan and Ramnath not to rob, but "to see the place".

He said when he went with Joshua Ramnath and Goolcharan to Curepe, they limed around for several hours before Goolcharan took them to Sampson's taxi and they got in.

He said he thought they were going back to El Socorro.

Bachan will return to the witness stand cross-examination when the trial resumes today.

Compare Bachan's reported statement that "he buss a man throat" with Ramnath's reported statement: "he claimed he saw Bachan slit Sampson's throat". There are issues of orthography, interpretation and translation in representing Bachan's Creole as Trinidadian Creole English and as Trinidadian Standard English as well. It is possible that the police's, court reporter's and journalist's versions could vary. As has been shown by Patrick and Buell (2000), the type of expertise among prosecution translator of Jamaican Creole, defence linguist and prosecution linguist varies. Given the range of interpretations demonstrated by Patrick and Buell, it is not a far-fetched proposition to imagine a similar or wider range of interpretations among the persons who render Bachan's spoken and written English. To date, access to the actual police and official verbatim court reporter's versions has not been possible. What happened eventually in the case? Bachan was found guilty of murder, and, on February 21, 2006, he was sentenced to hang.

The Piarco Case: Authenticity of a Document

In another case, example 2A, the authenticity of a document was challenged (Mills 2006a). In this case the authenticity of a tendered, computer-generated document was challenged by the defence attorney, who submitted this instance as one requiring the use of a computer expert by the state to "testify and explain". The issue of authenticity arose when, Borely, a chartered accountant (whose first name was not reported), attempted to refer to two documents purported to have been generated from the computer system at Maritime, an insurance company which employed some of the accused in the trial of persons alleged to have engaged in fraudulent activities during the construction of a new Piarco International Airport in Trinidad.

The defence attorney challenged the documents on the basis of "the law [which] bound the State to call technical witnesses to testify that the computer systems which produced the documents were functional and that the documents were without error". In previously documented forensic linguistics cases, the authenticity of documents is not based on the kind of evidence of technical witnesses described above, but on the basis of the evidence of forensic linguists who examine other issues such as authorship disputes. Such investigation analyses lexical, syntactical and discourse elements. Establishing whether the computer systems were functional and the documents were without error is not sufficient to establish the authenticity of the documents. Was the style of the document consistent with the style of Maritime documents? Could the authorship characteristics of the disputed document be linked to the known authorship characteristics of other Maritime computer-generated documents? Incidentally, the attempt to scientifically explore the idea of a linguistic "voice print" for speakers seems similar to the pursuit of the Holy Grail, and is no longer regarded as a reputable line of investigation (McMenamin 2002). However, attempts to determine authorship of written texts are more reputable and are capable of producing evidence for fact finding.

Example 2A

Frank Solomon, SC, objected to Borely looking at two sets of documents that were seized from Maritime General Insurance Co. Ltd and were in evidence.

He argued that the documents were computer generated and the law bound the State to call technical witnesses to testify that the computer systems which produced the documents were functional and that the documents were without error.

However, leading prosecuting attorney Gilbert Peterson, SC, expressed shock at the objection and Solomon's suggestion that the State subpoena someone from Maritime to testify that the computer generated documents were produced with a working computer system.

He argued that such evidence would be "self-incriminatory" and there should be a distinction between computer generated evidence from State witnesses and those seized from accused people or entities.

Defence attorney Desmond Allum, SC, joined Solomon and said the legislation should not be breached and if the State was having difficulty with the law, they should have gone to the attorney general to have it amended.

McNicolls overruled the objection.

Queen's Counsel Edward Jenkins later attempted to tender into evidence, through Borely, another document allegedly related to the first set that were argued over.

This too, was objected to by Solomon as he pointed out a discrepancy which questioned the authenticity of the document. When Jenkins attempted to explain, Solomon and defence attorney Vernon de Lima objected.

The defence attorney hammered this in as an example of why the State should call a computer expert to testify and explain.

The matter continues on Monday.

When the matter resumed, the judge ruled that the document was admissible. The newspaper report stated (see example 2B):

Example 2B

Queen's Counsel Edward Jenkins applied to get a document into evidence through Borely [an accountant].

Solomon objected and re-read his notes from Friday's sitting to try to convince McNicolls that the document was not what Borely said it was.

In response Deputy Director of Public Prosecutions Carla Browne-Antoine read her notes to show that Borely never said what the document was and its identity was argued over by the attorneys.

McNicolls said he listened extensively to arguments and there was no need for further submission on the admissibility of the document and overruled the defence's objections and allowed the document to be tendered into evidence.

However, even after the ruling, Solomon rose to have the notes from the court read to him and raised the issue again.

After about ten minutes of cross-referencing his notes with those of the court, McNicolls still allowed the document. (Mills 2006b)

Is there a case for the use of a forensic linguist as an expert witness in this case? In this instance the authenticity of a text was disputed, and the decision was based on the legal issue of admissible evidence. The issue of the authenticity of the text, however, was not addressed. Here the legal issue took precedence over the authenticity issue. Does this suggest a boundary for determining when recourse to the testimony of expert witnesses, including forensic linguists, is necessary or not? It seems that the establishment of admissibility of evidence takes precedence over questions relating to the relevance of the evidence. Here the boundary seems to be demarcated by the primacy of legal over non-legal issues.

State versus Sandy and Sandy: Suspicious Evidence

In another case, example 3, the evidence of the main witness was the turning point in the trial involving two brothers accused of murder. The witness's statement was viewed as "suspicious" and the trial was stopped. It should be noted, however, that the nature of the suspicion was based on questions not relating to the language or authorship of the statement. The term "suspicious" was used by the journalist. The director of public prosecutions stated that the disappearance and re-appearance of a warrant, claimed by the defence to have been mislaid (as an inducement to the witness to change his testimony between the preliminary inquiry and the trial), provided new information. He stated, "That information makes, in a very real sense, the evidence of Kenroy Bruno suspect, in that it cannot be rebutted that it may be as result of a powerful inducement, particularly when the witness had claimed that he did not know who had shot Haynes in a first statement to the police."

Interestingly, there were two statements by the state's main witness, one in which he is reported to have said he did not know who had shot the deceased, and another one in which he stated he had seen the accused brothers shoot the deceased. The services of a forensic linguist would be useful in comparing the authorship characteristics of the two statements. A forensic linguist could provide expert testimony as to whether the two statements were capable of being produced by the same author.

Example 3

The State yesterday discontinued murder charges against two Laventille brothers after deeming the evidence of its main witness as suspicious.

Director of Public Prosecutions Geoffrey Henderson informed Justice Devan Rampersad in the Port of Spain Third Criminal Court, Hall of Justice, of the State's decision to stop the trial.

The judge directed the foreman of the 12-member jury to return formal not-guilty verdicts.

Henderson said the indictment against Sean Sandy, 32, and Romel "Bumbles" Sandy, 34, was based on the evidence of Kenroy Bruno.

This was the second time the Sandy brothers have walked free on a murder charge.

In this case, defence attorneys Ian Brooks and Leon Gokool claimed the police had deliberately misplaced an outstanding warrant for Bruno's arrest on a charge of possession of cocaine for the purpose of trafficking, and used that as an inducement for him to implicate their client in the July 29, 2004 murder of Roger Haynes.

Haynes, 30, of Fairley Street, Tunapuna, was shot three times in the head by two men who approached his car near Sandy Trace.

Henderson admitted that the disclosure of the warrant had caused
the defence some anxiety and referred to Bruno's own testimony, during
the preliminary enquiry, where the witness stated that police officers
"took care of the warrant".

He said the defence had previously requested State attorneys investi-
gate the claim, but up until a few minutes before the matter was called
yesterday, police had reported that the warrant had been misplaced and
could not be found.

Confession Statement and Witness Credibility

In two other situations, the critical role of justices of the peace in
observing the taking of a witness's confession statement was stressed
(Swamber 2006), and the role of the police in determining the credibility of a witness was questioned (Lal-Beharie 2006). In the first situation, Sheldon Fraser was charged with the manslaughter of his best
friend. The dictated statement, which he had made in the presence of a
justice of the peace, contained a statement that he had been attacked
with a knife wielded by the deceased, but this information was not in
the written version. This information was revealed later in court by the
justice of the peace, and the accused was freed. A similar example
occurs in a second situation in which a lawyer challenged the police's
role in determining the credibility of an allegation. In that situation, the
claimed unreliability of an unsigned witness statement led to a police
decision not to proceed with a case, although an attorney commented
that it was not the role of the police to determine the credibility of witnesses (Lal-Beharie 2006).

These two situations demonstrate that both the justices of the peace
and the police have important roles in judgments made by others about
the credibility of witness statements, but they are not expected to be
judges. When such credibility is questioned in court, there is a role for
the forensic linguist in providing expert factual evidence, not commen-
tary on points of law. The expert factual evidence of the forensic linguist is limited to evidence that could help judicial officers and juries to
come to conclusions about disputed authorship or the different versions
of statements. Regarding the first situation, by comparing undisputed
samples of an author's spoken or written language with samples of disputed language purported to have been produced by disputed authors,

the forensic linguist can provide evidence as to the likelihood that an author could or could not produce disputed texts. In the second situation, since the statement was unsigned, but purported to have been made by a witness, the role of the forensic linguist is limited to assisting the court with determining questions of authorship not the credibility of the author.

Conclusion

The cited cases provide a sense of the scope of issues that may engage forensic linguists in the Caribbean. The issues are based on witness statements. In the examples cited, the scope of the forensic linguist is limited to questions of authorship or disputed authorship by establishing the basis for factual determinations rather than legal ones. As argued in examples 1, 1A and 1B, the forensic linguist's expertise in lexical, syntactical and pragmatic characteristics of texts produced by speakers/writers can be useful in such fact-finding efforts. Issues of lexicon, syntax and pragmatics are worth exploring in the context of the differences between varieties of language, between spoken and written statements, and between different versions of text or discourse, in so far as a corpus of such cases allows.

Examples 2A and 2B relate to the authenticity of texts. The question that arose was whether in matters relating to the legality of evidence and the authenticity of evidence there is a basis for establishing boundaries and protocols for the precedence of one kind of evidence over another. If the response to such a question is that the admissibility of evidence takes precedence over the relevance of the evidence, then there may be a basis for using legal rather than non-legal facts to demarcate the role of the forensic linguist. This response can help to determine the boundaries for the role of forensic linguists. Example 3 refers to authorship and credibility issues relating to texts and the role of the forensic linguist in assisting the court with matters of fact, not legality. Of course, such assistance as the forensic linguist provides can help the court to determine the relevance, and ultimately the admissibility, of evidence.

A corpus of witness statements and the principles and lessons derived from comparing samples of texts can provide benchmarks and expert opinion for making informed judgements about disputed witness statements which contain disputed and undisputed versions. Such a corpus can contribute to the study of Caribbean language through the development of an applied science of language use and usage in the courtroom context. The findings about language use by witnesses are one area of potential research in Caribbean forensic linguistics. Other scholars are interested in questions of interpretation, the language of instructions to juries, and the language of judicial officers, attorneys and so on. But at the heart of language matters in the courtroom are the nature and characteristics of evidence contained in witness statements.

Forensic linguistics has a role to play in the determination of factual matters of language use, but there is another reciprocal role for applied linguistics in relation to Caribbean language. This role lies in the determination of whether descriptive and theoretical linguistic knowledge of Caribbean speakers is influenced or modified in the context of the courtroom. Is there any reason to suppose that the texts produced by speakers/hearers could vary on the basis of their location in a courtroom setting? Forensic linguistics in the Caribbean can go beyond fact finding in legal cases to include fact finding about Caribbean language.

References

Ali, I. 2006. Mayaro Murder Accused Claims Accomplice Killed Taxi-Driver. *Trinidad Daily Express*. February 14.

Bahaw, D. 2006. State Stops Murder Case: Evidence Suspicious. *Trinidad Daily Express*. June 14.

Blackwell, S. 2003. Mute Pleads Guilty to Murder by Mistake. *Trinidad Daily Express*. July 9. http://web.bham.ac.uk/forensic/news/03/mute.html (accessed July 24, 2006).

Crystal, D. 1997. *The Cambridge Encyclopedia of Language*. 2nd ed. Cambridge: Cambridge University Press.

Eades, D. 1994. Forensic Linguistics in Australia. *Forensic Linguistics* 1 (2): 113–32.

Evans, S. 2005. The Use of Court Clerks as "Makeshift" Legal Interpreters in St Lucian Courts. Paper presented at the seventh Biennial Conference on Forensic Linguistics/Language and the Law, Cardiff University, Wales, July 1–4.

Forrester, C. 2005. Discourse of Time in the Jamaican Courtroom: Creole-Speaking Witness Meets English-Speaking Counsel. Paper presented at the seventh Biennial Conference on Forensic Linguistics/Language and the Law, Cardiff University, Wales, July 1–4.

International Association of Forensic Linguists. http://www.iafl.org/ (accessed February 24, 2006).

Komter, M.L. 2002. The Suspect's Own Words: The Treatment of Written Statements in Dutch Courtrooms. *Forensic Linguistics* 9 (2): 168–92.

Lal-Beharie, G. 2006. Lawyer: Listen to Vernon Paul. *Trinidad Daily Express*. February 1.

Marks, M. 2003a. Mute Man Acquitted in Trinidad. *Trinidad Daily Express*. July 17. http://www.margaret-marks.com/Transblawg/archives/2003_07. html (accessed July 24, 2006).

———. 2003b. Mute Pleads Guilty to Murder by Mistake. *Trinidad Daily Express*. July 9. http://www.margaret-marks.com/Transblawg/archives/ 2003_07.html (accessed July 24, 2006).

McMenamin, G.R. 2002. *Forensic Linguistics: Advances in Forensic Stylistics*. Boca Raton: CRC Press.

Mills, H. 2006a. State and Defence in Row Over Documents. *Trinidad Daily Express*. February 18.

———. 2006b. Magistrate Allows Evidence after Defence Objections. *Trinidad Daily Express*. February 21.

Patrick, P.L., and S.W. Buell. 2000. Competing Creole Transcripts on Trial. *Essex Research Reports in Linguistics* 32: 103–32.

Rock, F. 2001. The Genesis of a Witness Statement. *Forensic Linguistics* 8 (2): 44–72.

Salkie, R. 1995. *Text and Discourse Analysis*. London: Routledge.

Shields-Brodber, K. 2002. The Prosecution Now Calls John Doe. Paper presented at the Society for Caribbean Linguistics Fourteenth Biennial Conference, University of the West Indies, St Augustine, Trinidad, August 14–17.

Steele, G.A. 2005. The Language of the Law and the Interpretation of the Law: Issues of Language and Communication. Paper presented at the seventh Biennial Conference on Forensic Linguistics/Language and the Law, Cardiff University, Wales, July 1–4.

———. 2007. Course Content for the Language of the Law and the Interpretation of the Law. In *Language and the Law: International Outlooks*, ed. K. Kredens and S. Roszkowski. Bern: Peter Lang.

Swamber, K. 2006. "Best Friend" Freed of Manslaughter Charge. *Trinidad Daily Express*. February 17.

Tiersma, Peter. N.d. What Is Forensic Linguistics? http://www.languageand law.org/forensic.htm (accessed February 24, 2006).

Tyrwhitt-Drake, H. 2003. Massaging the Evidence: The "Over-working" of Witness Statements in Civil Cases. *International Journal of Speech Language and the Law* 10 (2): 227–54.

Webster's Forensic Linguistics Home Page. http://web.bham.ac.uk/forensic/ index.html (accessed February 24, 2006).

Glossary

Ante-mortem: Preceding death.

Ante-mortem data: The biological and physical profile of a person before death.

BIOS (Basic Input/Output System): Refers to the programme code residing in some type of computer memory that imitates hardware component testing when the computer is first powered or before the operating system is loaded.

Computer forensics: Also known as digital forensics, this is a specialty area within forensic science in which scientific principles and computer technologies are applied to the legal problem of digital evidence.

Creole: A variety of language whose lexicon (or vocabulary), phonology (sound system) and grammar may be shared with another language but which may have distinct rules and patterns of use among its speakers and writers from those used by native speakers and writers of the related language. An English-lexicon Creole, for example, such as Trinidadian Creole English, shares a lexicon or vocabulary with English, but the rules and patterns of use governing the meaning, spelling, pronunciation and function of those words may be different or represent a variation of lexical (word), phonological (sound) or grammatical use. Some creoles, such as St Lucian Creole, may share a lexicon with another language that is quite distinct, such as French, as well as another language, such as English.

De-briefing: A meeting called to review all activities surrounding the mass casualty or mass fatality incident.

Digital evidence: Evidence that resides in computer and digital devices or digital media which is extracted and analysed in a manner admissible in the court of law.

Disaster victim identification: The process by which victims are identified whilst utilizing both police and scientific investigative techniques.

Discourse: Refers to spoken or written language used in statements. It also refers to language used when there is interaction between two or more speakers/writers. In formal linguistics, discourse also refers to the structural organization of spoken and written utterances beyond the sentence unit. It includes the entire body of opening, main and closing utterances connected together by topic, theme or various linking elements.

Discourse analysis: A field of study as well as an analytical method that is used to study the patterns and organization of turn sequences in naturally occurring speech, or in written texts used to represent naturally occurring speech.

Discourse/discoursal features: Elements of discourse which create links or coherence and cohesion or unity in utterances longer than a sentence and/or involving interactions between two or more speakers and writers.

Disk editor: A software tool with a graphical user interface that allows users to view, and to modify (edit), individual bytes of computer disk or individual computer files.

File system: A part of the computer operating system that specifies how data are organized as files, and how files are stored and accessed, popular file systems include FAT and NTFS on Microsoft Windows system, Ext 2/3 on Linux system, and UFS on BSD-Unix system.

Forensic anthropology: The application of the science of physical anthropology and human osteology (the study of the human skeleton) in a legal setting, most often in criminal cases where the victim's remains are more or less skeletonized. A forensic anthropologist can also assist in the identification of deceased individuals whose remains are decomposed, burned, mutilated or otherwise unrecognizable.

Forensic linguist: The term for a linguist who has had training in forensic linguistic analysis and who has knowledge and competence in one or more branches of linguistics. A forensic linguist can provide expert evidence on matters of linguistic fact which may assist a court and its officers in determining the factual nature of language evidence.

Forensic pathology: A branch of medicine concerned with determining cause of death, usually for criminal law cases and civil law cases in some jurisdictions. The word forensics is derived from the Latin *forensis* meaning "public" or "forum". The word "pathology" literally means "study of suffering".

Geographic information systems (GIS): An organized collection of computer hardware, software, geographic data and personnel designed to efficiently capture, store, update, manipulate, analyse and display all forms of geographically referenced information.

Hash value: A small value computed by applying a mapping algorithm to the contents of a file which can be used to uniquely identify the source file with near certainty; that is, a digital fingerprint of the source file.

Incident command system: A standardized organizational structure used to command, control and coordinate the use of resources and personnel that have responded to the scene of an emergency.

Lexical analysis: A tool used in forensic linguistics to study words used in language. It is a method of linguistic analysis which identifies and compares the patterns and rules governing the characteristics, frequency, choice, and use of words by speakers and writers.

Linguistics: The name of the academic discipline that concerns itself with the systematic study and description of human language.

Mass casualty: An event which generates, or has the potential to generate, a sufficient number of victims to overwhelm the existing emergency services' ability to adequately manage patients.

MD5: Message Digest Algorithm 5 is a widely used algorithm designed by Ron Rivest in 1991 that computes a 128-bit hash value.

Mitochondrial DNA (mtDNA): DNA that is considered within the mitochondria, one of the cellular organelles. In humans, mitochondrial DNA appears to be 100 per cent inherited from the mother, and maternal lineage can be traced back hundreds of generations based on studies of mtDNA. Unlike the DNA in the nucleus, which changes by fifty per cent with each generation, there is very little change to the mitochondr-ial DNA. Thus, every mutation in mitochondria can be easily measured.

Peri-mortem: Occurring at the time of death.

Police record of interview: The term applied to witness statements in Australia.

Post-mortem: After death.

Post-mortem data: The biological and physical profile of a person after death which is gathered from forensic investigations.

RAM: Random access memory, a type of computer storage that uses integrated circuitry to load applications and associated data when they are being run on a computer.

Regular expression: A concise notation composed of alphanumeric characters and special symbols that can be used to specify character strings of interest during keyword searches using a software tool.

SHA1: Secure Hash Algorithm 1 computes a hash value of 160 bits and is one of a series of SHA algorithms published by the United States NIST (National Institute of Standards and Technology).

Stand down: This term means to cease operations surrounding the mass casualty or mass fatality incident.

Syntactic analysis: A tool used in forensic linguistics to study the gram-matical structures of language. It is a method of linguistic analysis that identifies and compares the structures and rules that govern the order of strings of utterances used by speakers and writers

Text: Refers to the language used in statements as, for example, in wit-ness statements. It also refers to language that represents what a speaker or writer produces.

Trinidadian Standard English: A variety of English which is accepted as the official language of instruction. It is expected to be used as the stan-dard variety in matters of education, business, commerce, and law and literacy. It often enjoys a degree of prestige not usually accorded Trinidadian Creole English, but this differential status is not shared by all users of the two languages.

Windows registry: A hierarchical database made up of keys and values and used in Microsoft Windows operating systems which store information including the settings, configuration, user profiles, and applications installed.

Witness statement: Refers to an oral or written statement given by a witness and recorded by a police officer and signed by the witness which may be used as evidence in a court matter.

Write blocker: A piece of hardware or software connecting the storage media (for example, computer hard disk) and a computer which prevents any modification to the storage media while reading its content.

Index

Response Team procedures, 9
footwear analysis, 5
La Belle Drug Murder Case, 49–50
misidentified female remains, 44, 48
US Forensic Database, 46–47
US National Institute of Science and Technology, 61
University of the West Indies, forensic science, 51

Venezuala, 76
victim identification
biological database sources, 13–14
counselling support, 19
dental records, 14, 15
DNA analysis, 2, 14, 15, 30, 34, 36, 47
by family members, 18–19
fingerprints, 14
and forensic anthropology, 3, 29–30
internal physical evidence, 15
mass casualty response plan, 15–19
medical records, 14, 15
operational stages in disaster management, 13–15

personal effects, 14
photographs, 14
stages of, 10
toxicological findings, 15
worldwide protocols, 9
visual identification, in victim identification, 14–15

Willey, O., 40
witness statements
authorship of, determining, 117, 120–21
confession statements, 127–28
in Dutch legal system, 120
forensic linguistics and, 5–6, 116–30
justices of the peace, role of, 127
newspaper reporting of, 119
suspicious evidence, 125–27
World Trade Center attack, 2, 34, 47
write-blockers, 61

X-rays, 34
of teeth, ante-mortem, 47
X-Ways computer software, 60

Contributors

BASIL A. REID is Lecturer in Archaeology, Department of History, University of the West Indies, St Augustine, Trinidad and Tobago. He has worked on pre-Columbian sites in Jamaica, Barbados, Haiti, and Trinidad and Tobago, and his major research interests are the pre-Columbian history of the Caribbean, archaeology, and geoinformatics and forensics in the Caribbean. He has published in a variety of peer-reviewed publications such as the *Journal of Caribbean History, Caribbean Quarterly* and *Caribbean Geography*. He has also written several papers on forensic anthropology for popular audiences. He is the editor of *Archaeology and Geoinformatics: Case Studies from the Caribbean* and author of *Myths and Realities of Caribbean History*.

NAZIR ALLADIN is Director of Campus Information Technology Services, University of the West Indies, St Augustine, Trinidad and Tobago. He has presented papers locally and internationally on the SunGard Banner and Oracle PeopleSoft applications. He has been engaged in a number of consultancies which have facilitated the growth and development of organizations throughout Trinidad and Tobago and the wider Caribbean.

CHERYL A. CORBIN is Director of the Forensic Sciences Centre, Office of the Attorney General, Barbados. Ms Corbin is actively involved in the training of all law enforcement personnel on the island in matters of evidence, chain of custody and general forensic procedures, as well as instruction to the local academic institutions. She has successfully completed coordinating two projects under the United Nations Drug Control Programme and the European Union Development Programme, as well as providing forensic consultancy services to the wider Caribbean region.

SHEAU-DONG LANG is Associate Professor in the School of Electrical Engineering and Computer Science at the University of Central Florida, Orlando, Florida. His research interests include algorithm design and analysis, databases, information storage and retrieval, network security, and digital forensics. Dr Lang has published over eighty research articles, supervised five doctoral candidates in computer science and is the coordinator for the University of Central Florida's Master of Science degree in digital forensics.

PARRIS LYEW-AYEE is Director of the Mona GeoInformatics Institute, University of the West Indies, Mona, Jamaica. His active research interests include natural hazards analyses, karst geomorphology, terrain signature diagnoses, Martian rock breakdown analyses, transport systems modelling, geocomputational modelling, geospatial planning for businesses, GPS systems, and web mapping and crime modelling.

JERRY MELBYE is Professor of Forensic Anthropology, Texas State University–San Marcos; Fellow of the American Academy of Forensic Sciences; Diplomat of the American Board of Forensic Anthropology; and a consultant to law enforcement agencies in Texas.

TREVOR MODESTE is Superintendent of Police, Royal Grenada Police Force. He has studied a vast range of crime-solving techniques throughout his career and has steadily upgraded his expertise and skills by attending several forensic workshops and seminars in Grenada, Barbados, Jamaica, Trinidad, Belize, Japan, India and Metro Dade Miami (Florida). Superintendent Modeste was awarded the Most Excellent Order of the British Empire in 2006 for services rendered to the Royal Grenada Police Force.

GODFREY A. STEELE is Senior Lecturer in Communication Studies, Department of Liberal Arts, University of the West Indies, St Augustine, Trinidad and Tobago. His research interests are the applied use of communication in health, legal, conflict management and communication education, and his projects include communication and conflict management, communication and culture, Creole language use in the courtroom, a health communication textbook and a reader. His paper on course content for language and the law was published in *Language and the Law: International Outlooks* in 2007.

CARL MARTIN WINSKOG is a forensic pathologist in South Australia. He is the former Head of Pathology, Forensic Sciences Centre, Office of the Attorney General, Barbados. His principal areas of interests are in the use of and the development of computer assisted tomography (CAT scan) in forensic medicine, disaster victim identification, crime-scene investigations and forensic photography. Dr Winskog has published papers in the area of virtual autopsies as well as lung injuries. His international assignments include that of chief forensic pathologist for disaster victim identification teams in Thailand in 2005 and in Barbados in 2006.

www.ingramcontent.com/pod-product-compliance
Lightning Source LLC
Chambersburg PA
CBHW080424270326
41929CB00018B/3157